DOUBLE TAKE
Two sides One story

Tutankhamun's TOMB

ALAN MACDONALD

In memory of my father who took me to see Tutankhamun

This story is based, as much as possible, on primary source material - the words and
pictures of the people that witnessed the events described. Whilst it is not possible to
know the exact thoughts, feelings and motives of all the people involved, the book aims
to give an insight into the experience of the events, based on the available evidence.

Scholastic Children's Books
Commonwealth House, 1–19 New Oxford Street,
London, WC1A 1NU, UK
A division of Scholastic Ltd
London ~ New York ~ Toronto ~ Sydney ~ Auckland
Mexico City ~ New Delhi ~ Hong Kong

Published in the UK by Scholastic Ltd, 2003

ISBN 0 439 98238 3

Printed and bound in Denmark
by Nørhaven Paperback A/S

Cover image supplied by Getty Images

2 4 6 8 10 9 7 5 3

Contents

Prologue

IT WAS ONLY A SMALL HOLE – not much bigger than a fist – but wide enough to insert a flickering candle into the darkness beyond. Through that small hole the two Englishmen – Howard Carter and Lord Carnarvon – caught their first glimpse of wonders not seen for over 3,000 years.

In the dark at first they could make out little more than shadows. Then the shadows began to take on shape and form in the candlelight. Three great golden couches, carved with the heads and claws of strange beasts. To the right were two black statues of a proud king, each one as big as a man, standing guard over the room. Against a wall a pile of enormous chariots lay in a confused heap. Everywhere lay caskets and vases, golden thrones, beds and beautifully carved chests that contained wonders they could only guess at. All their lives Carter and Carnarvon had dreamed of a moment like this – now they could scarcely believe the evidence of their eyes.

Introduction

HOWARD CARTER and Lord Carnarvon are remembered as the discoverers of Tutankhamun's tomb. But the truth is, the find that stunned the world on 26 November 1922 almost never happened.

Carter and Carnarvon had joined forces as early as 1907 in the search for ancient tombs and treasures. From early on the ultimate aim of their partnership was to dig in the legendary Valley of the Kings, which housed the tombs of the great Pharaohs. But when their chance finally came, luck seemed to desert them. Five barren years brought nothing but failure. In 1922 they came very close to giving up. Howard Carter persuaded his employer, Lord Carnarvon, to give him one last chance to find the lost tomb and within weeks of arriving in Egypt he found a hidden staircase, which led down to a sealed door.

The tale has all the elements of the best adventure stories – two men searching against the odds to find a tomb that nobody else believed in. It's a story that brings together the lure of gold and the ancient secrets of Egypt. It offers us the thrill of the treasure hunt, the mummy in the tomb and the legend of a sinister curse.

Yet there is another story that few people know – the story of the two men who found Tutankhamun. Carter and Carnarvon were not a partnership made in heaven. They were an odd couple, as different as chalk and cheese. One was a brittle, self-made man, with little education and no money. The other was a wealthy Lord, schooled at Eton and with a passion of racehorses and fast cars.

United in the search for Tutankhamun's tomb, their differences eventually led to arguments and, just four months after the triumph of the discovery, Carter and Carnarvon's relationship reached breaking point. Things sank so low that Carter threw his patron out of his house, telling him never to return. Only weeks after the row Carnarvon was dead, leaving Carter to carry on alone. The discovery, which had promised such a golden future, threatened to become a curse. Carter's work on the tomb ran into a storm of politics. Pushed to breaking point, he eventually walked out, leaving Tutankhamun's tomb closed and padlocked.

This is a story that, as Carnarvon's sister, Lady Burghclere, said, opens like the tale of Aladdin and ends like a Greek tragedy. At its heart is a boy-king who, even today, remains shrouded in mystery. On that remarkable day in 1922, when Carter and Carnarvon caught their first glimpse of gold, they had no idea of how their lives were about to change…

The Call of Egypt

1866 – 1906

THE ROAD AHEAD was straight as an arrow and George Stanhope Herbert, 5th Earl of Carnarvon, applied his foot to the accelerator. His destination was the town of Bad Schwalbach in Germany where his wife, Lady Almina, would be waiting to meet him.

In his native England cars were still regarded as dangerous contraptions and only allowed to drive at a snail's pace of six miles an hour. Even then a man had to walk in front waving a red flag as a warning to pedestrians and horse carriages. Carnarvon was scornful of such caution. On several occasions he'd been brought before a magistrate for driving at *"frightening speeds"* of up to 20 miles an hour. He was not a man who wanted to live life at a snail's pace. At the age of 35 he was impatient for adventure.

Suddenly, as the car sped over the crest of a hill, he

saw that disaster lay just ahead. A bullock cart had halted right across the road. The owners were attempting to move the stubborn beasts but now they turned and gaped stupidly at the car speeding towards them. There was no time to brake – the car was going too fast. Carnarvon had only a matter of seconds to make a decision. At moments of danger like this, he found he was surprisingly calm and clear-headed. He calculated that his only chance of avoiding a head-on crash was to try to swerve round the cart and pass it on the grass verge. Trotman, his chauffeur, was now sitting bolt upright in the passenger seat, his face deathly pale.

The bullock drivers fled from the road uttering cries of terror. Carnarvon kept his nerve and turned the wheel sharply as he reached the cart. He only saw the pile of rocks at the last moment and heard the loud explosion as they ripped through the tyres. Then the car was turning a somersault in the air and he had a brief view of the tilting sky before everything went blank.

Trotman had been flung clear on to the grass in the collision. Bruised and shaken, he staggered to his feet to see what had happened. The car had come to rest upside down across a ditch with its wheels spinning. Smoke and flames were issuing from the engine. There was no sign of Lord Carnarvon. Trotman guessed that his master was underneath the car, but whether dead or alive, he couldn't tell.

Clambering into the ditch, Trotman summoned all his strength and tried to heave the car on to its side. It was a superhuman task for one man, but the car's body was lightweight and the chauffeur was desperate. At the third attempt he got the car to roll over like a helpless turtle.

Carnarvon was still in the driving seat but Trotman was shaken by what he saw. His master's body was caked in mud from head to foot, the head lolling on one side. Carnarvon's face was swollen with ugly bruising and there seemed to be something wrong with the shape of his jaw. If he were alive it would be a miracle.

Trotman got his hands underneath his master's body and managed to drag it clear on to the grass. He loosened Carnarvon's clothing but when he listened, he couldn't detect a heartbeat. He threw some water on to his master's face to try to revive him. Some distance away he could see a group of farm workers in a field. He ran towards them, waving his arms and shouting.

Carnarvon didn't die that day on the road in Germany in 1901, but his life was altered for ever. By a strange twist of fate, the accident led him to Egypt and the discovery that would make his name famous throughout the world.

Up to this point, Carnarvon had been carefree and idle, travelling wherever he pleased. Born into a wealthy aristocratic English family, he was labelled a "delicate" child and spoiled as a result. While his father was alive his title was Lord Porchester and his nickname, "Porchy", stuck for the rest of his life. Porchy's father was a busy statesman and his mother died when he was only nine. Porchy was left in the care of two eccentric aunts: Lady Gwendolen Herbert and Lady Portsmouth. Their ideas about bringing up children were completely opposed. Aunt Gwendolen generally gave her nephew anything he wanted while strict Lady Portsmouth usually took it away again. Once, when Porchy broke a window, his Aunt Gwendolen gave him half a crown to cheer him up. Another time she let him have a saw to play with. Lady Portsmouth promptly took away the dangerous weapon and hung it on the schoolroom wall for safe-keeping.

School – at Eton – didn't interest Carnarvon much. At 19 he moved on to university at Cambridge. He was a born adventurer and wanted to see the world. At the age of 21 he set off on a round-the-world cruise on a yacht. He never made it right round the globe but he did cause quite a stir in Argentina when he invited the President to dine on his yacht. In the following years he travelled to Japan and Australia, drove motor cars and owned racehorses. He married Almina in 1895 on his 29th birthday and children followed: a son, Henry, and daughter, Evelyn. This carefree existence ended on that fateful day when his car went off the road in Germany.

Carnarvon had plenty of time to think back over his life as he lay in his hospital bed. The accident left him with a broken wrist, severe burns and a badly injured jaw. He was lucky to be alive but there was a price to pay. For the rest of his days Carnarvon would be crippled by painful headaches and bouts of illness. His life of fast cars, racehorses and globe-trotting was over. The doctors did their best, but admitted their patient would never regain full health. It was a bitter blow for someone as active as Carnarvon. His breathing suffered most. The doctor suggested the damp English winters were bad for him. Maybe he should go abroad – somewhere warm. Egypt for example?

Carnarvon arrived in Egypt in the winter of 1903, two years after his accident.

He was 37 years old. What could an English lord with a taste for adventure find to do in Egypt? He could travel around like all the other foreign tourists, seeing the pyramids and the tombs. He could cruise the Nile or sip tea in some of the best hotels in Cairo or Luxor. But it wouldn't be long before a man like Porchy would be bored to death. What he needed was a hobby – something to throw himself into.

Since his schooldays, Carnarvon had developed a passion for collecting. At Eton he had searched antique shops for fine china, which he'd kept in his desk. So it was no surprise that archaeology caught his imagination. What is an archaeologist, after all? Someone who collects relics of the past. Better than that, someone who digs for buried treasure. The writer Rudyard Kipling once summed up the life of an archaeologist: *"It furnishes a scholarly pursuit with all the excitement of a gold prospector's life."* Knowledge combined with the thrill of the hunt. It was just the adventure Carnarvon needed. He knew enough about Egypt to know that the tombs of fabulous Pharaohs had been discovered there. In time he might even build up a collection of Egyptian art for his family home at Highclere Castle. All these things attracted Carnarvon, but most of all he wanted *something to do* during the long winter months in Egypt. Excavation appealed to him. He would throw himself into it and see what turned up.

Unfortunately it wasn't as simple a matter as buying a spade and choosing a spot to dig. In Egypt at the turn of the century archaeologists had to apply to the government authorities for a site to dig. Archaeology in this period was dominated by the French, British, Italians and Americans. Egypt itself was occupied by the British army and had little control over its own destiny. Luckily Carnarvon had a friend, Sir William Garstin, who encouraged him in his new hobby. Garstin was an adviser to the Cairo Ministry of Public Works – which handed out archaeological sites through its Department of Antiquities. Carnarvon got his first taste of excavation in 1907 through Garstin's efforts. The English lord wrote later:

I may say at this period I knew nothing whatever about excavating. I suppose with the idea of keeping me out of mischief, as well as keeping me employed, I was allotted a site at the top of Sheikh Abel Gurna. I had scarcely been operating for 24 hours when we suddenly struck what seemed to be an untouched burial pit... There for six weeks, enveloped in clouds of dust, I stuck to it day in and day out.

Actually, Porchy didn't *"stick to it"* personally. He was too weak for spade-work (*"I only weigh 8st 12lbs and cannot go up."*). He sat in a screened cage, protected from the flies and dust, while his team of Egyptian workmen did the digging. Some days later he was joined by his wife, Almina, who was, as one writer described, *"dressed for a garden party rather than the desert. With charming patent leather high-heeled shoes and a good deal of jewellery flashing in the sunlight."* This was excavation with tea and servants.

The results of his first dig were pretty dismal. The burial pit turned out to be unfinished, though Carnarvon did find a single mummified cat in its case. (Egyptians regarded cats as sacred animals and used to mummify them after their death.) The cat was given a home in Cairo Museum, but it was a poor reward for six weeks of toil in the baking sun.

Yet he was by no means put off. *"This utter failure,"* he said, *"instead of disheartening me had the effect of making me keener than ever."* The English lord had tasted the pleasures of the hunt. What's more, he was a gambler. Even if he hadn't found anything the first time, the next time – or the time after – he thought he might be lucky. It was just a matter of knowing where to look. And for that, it was dawning on Carnarvon, he needed the help of an expert.

Typically, he went to the top man for advice. The Frenchman Gaston Maspero was the all-powerful Director of the Department of Antiquities. As it happened, Maspero did know of a man he could recommend. There was an Englishman called Howard Carter who at present was scratching a living painting watercolours for tourists. Carnarvon was doubtful – he had no use for a penniless, out-of-work artist. But further enquiries revealed that Carter had worked for Maspero as an Inspector of Antiquities until he lost his job after an unpleasant incident. It's quite likely that Carnarvon had heard the rumours about Carter, who had a reputation for being stubborn and hotheaded. While an inspector, he had ordered his guards to attack a group of French tourists at a place called Saqqara, and had resigned as a result. Still, Maspero recommended the young man highly and Carnarvon didn't know anyone else who was suitable. Perhaps he would give this man Carter a chance.

The Outsider

1876 – 1905

HOWARD CARTER WAS BORN in Swaffham, Norfolk, in 1876, the son of Samuel Carter, an artist who painted animal pictures for the *London Illustrated News*. Howard was the youngest of a large family. His superior elder brothers always spoke of him as *"our younger brother"*. Carter later said, *"I received from them a lot of good training and at times sixpenny- or threepenny-bits if I allowed them to pick me up by my hair, or if I washed their brushes and scraped their palettes."*

From the start Carter was trained in drawing and painting, sketching pet parrots, cats and *"snappy, smelly lap-dogs"* for his father's customers. His education was sadly lacking as his parents kept him out of school because of his poor health. Maybe if Carter had been able to make friends and join in sports at an early age, he would have been better at dealing with people. Instead, at the tender age of 15, he was pushed out into the world to make his living. "*It is said that nature thrusts some of us into the world miserably incomplete*," said Carter, bitterly. All his life he would suffer from the feeling that he started from a disadvantage. But what he lacked in education or self-confidence he would make up for with sheer hard work and steely determination.

As a boy, Carter first fell under the spell of Egypt when he visited local Didlington Hall, the home of Lord and Lady Amherst. The Carters lived in London but spent their summers in Norfolk where young Howard wandered the villages with his paints and easel. Several of Samuel Carter's portraits hung in Didlington Hall and before long Lord Amherst took an interest in the artistic talent of 15-year-old Howard. Lord Amherst owned one of the finest Egyptian collections in the country. The young Carter was fascinated by pictures of chariots and jackal-headed gods. As someone who had never even been away to school, Carter felt a deep longing to visit this strange, mysterious country.

His chance came earlier than he expected. In 1891 the Egypt Exploration Fund were looking for an artist to go on their next expedition and Lady Amherst recommended Carter for the job. At the age of 17, Howard Carter set off by himself from London's Victoria Station to travel to Egypt. Any excitement he felt was overshadowed by loneliness and anxiety. He didn't know anyone where he was going and couldn't speak a word of the language. What on earth did he think he was doing?

Yet from the day of his arrival in Egypt, Carter never looked back. He may have been young and awkward, but he showed a real talent for drawing and painting. What's more, he didn't mind hard work. Carter was lucky enough to work for Flinders Petrie – the greatest archaeologist of his day. There was hardly a place in Egypt where Petrie hadn't dug and made important discoveries. With his ragged clothes and hair standing on end, Petrie prided himself on living simply and saving money. *"We eat no better than the natives, after all, we don't work any harder,"* he warned Carter. The young artist got his education from the great man.

Howard Carter found that he loved Egypt and his drawing skills were useful in archaeology. By a happy accident, he had found his life's work.

By the age of 30 Carter was a rising star in the small world of archaeology. As a Chief Inspector for the Department of Antiquities, Carter was responsible for supervising all excavations in Upper Egypt. The penniless Englishman who had arrived in Egypt with nothing but a sketchbook was now a man to be reckoned with. He had a comfortable salary of 400 Egyptian pounds a year and a house on the west bank of Luxor that he nicknamed "Castle Carter". Best of all, his job gave him the chance to do what he loved best – search for Egyptian tombs and burial sites.

Carter had been a surprise choice for the job and the quick-tempered Englishman had put a few noses out of joint. But his superior, Gaston Maspero, recognized his talent. *"I find him very active, a very good young man, a little obstinate..."* wrote Maspero.

"Obstinate" was the word that followed Carter about all his life. It was his stubbornness that eventually cost him his job.

Carter had been an inspector for six years when he was stationed at Saqqara in northern Egypt. The trouble blew up on 8 January 1905. In many ways it was a ridiculous incident, but the consequences for Carter were no laughing matter.

The French tourists had arrived in the afternoon at a rest house, one of the government properties used as visitor centres for tourists. There were about 15 of the Frenchmen and they'd stayed drinking and talking loudly for around an hour. Eventually they decided they would like to visit the local monuments. The local tourist attraction was the Serapeum, a large underground chamber where sacred bulls were buried. It was an impressive, rather eerie place and the French tourists were keen to see it.

On their arrival at the Serapeum, an argument broke out when the tourists were asked to buy tickets. Eventually most of them paid for tickets and the whole group entered the burial chamber. Inside they found themselves almost in darkness. When they demanded candles and learned none were provided, they became angry. The Department of Antiquities employed *gaffirs* or local guards to protect its property and some of these were jostled when the tourists demanded their money back. Things were getting out of hand and someone was sent to fetch Carter.

By the time Carter arrived, tempers were coming to the boil. The party of tourists had returned to the rest house in an attempt to get their money back. They had turned out the *gaffirs* and refused to leave. Carter found one door barricaded and was understandably furious.

Forcing his way into the house, he found the tourists all talking at once. Carter refused to refund their ticket money and bluntly told them to leave. His men had been mistreated and he felt he was dealing with a drunken rabble.

Insults were exchanged and before long a fight broke out. According to Carter, one of the Frenchmen *"struck a* gaffir *with his fist in the face"* without reason, knocking him down. The same man took a swing at Carter. Furniture was broken and cuts and bruises were suffered on both sides. Finally Carter ordered his men to drive the tourists out of the door. Using their long truncheons, the guards beat the French party into retreat – with one of the tourists injured in the fight. The visitors left with dark threats to inform the police, having taken Carter's name and rank.

Carter made his own report to the police and demanded that the culprits be arrested. On the face of it, he'd acted quite reasonably. He had only defended his men and the Department's property. Yet the incident could be looked at from two sides. The French version of events was that they had been attacked by Egyptian guards, armed with truncheons. The order for the attack had been given by Carter. Put like that, it didn't sound so reasonable.

The papers got hold of the story and turned it into a local scandal. Letters flew back and forth. The Department of Antiquities was embarrassed by the whole affair. While Carter's boss, Gaston Maspero, sympathized with his young inspector; he also had French tourism to think about. It was agreed that the whole messy business could be cleared up if Carter would just offer an apology and express his regret.

That might have been that. Carter's friends advised him to swallow his pride. Apologize. Everyone knew he was in the right but the important thing was to act diplomatically and keep his job – for there was little doubt that Carter's job was on the line now.

But Howard Carter wasn't a man to back down when he believed he was right. In his view he was the one who had been insulted and attacked. His men had been pushed and punched before they defended themselves. Why should he pretend that he was in the wrong?

It's easy to see Carter's point of view. But whatever the rights and wrongs of the case, an apology was needed to lay the matter to rest. Someone had to be the scapegoat and Carter was the obvious choice. Others might have accepted the injustice with a shrug of the shoulders. But not Carter. Pride and obstinacy ruled him. He would not apologize to anyone.

Two weeks went by and the situation was quietly smoothed over by his employers. Nevertheless, his stubbornness wasn't forgiven. He would have to pay. On 17 February another letter arrived from Gaston Maspero. Carter read it with a heavy heart. He was to keep his job but he would be transferred to Tanta in the Nile Delta – a sleepy backwater of Egypt where life would pass him by. Carter felt hurt and betrayed. He wrote back to Maspero:

> *I may say that I feel the humiliation to an exceeding extent. The treatment I have received after I have carried out my duty which has always been my endeavour is inconceivable...*

Carter asked for three-and-a-half months' leave due to the strain of work. Within six months of returning to his post at Tanta, he resigned. He didn't accept life's trials easily and burned with indignation. If the Department didn't appreciate his talents, then they didn't deserve him.

Carter kept his pride, but that was about all he had left. He had arrived in Egypt as a penniless outsider and now he was right back where he started. Just when it looked as if his career was on the rise, he found himself left out in the cold. While he licked his wounds he went back to his old trade, painting watercolours of local scenes for wealthy tourists. At the age of 31, the man who would make one of the greatest finds in history felt his life was a failure.

Carnarvon

In the Valley of the Kings

1907 – 1922

I<small>F</small> L<small>ORD</small> C<small>ARNARVON</small> <small>HEARD</small> about Carter's spot of trouble at Saqqara, he soon forgot about it. His new "hired man" turned out to be everything he'd hoped for. The partnership started out as a marriage of convenience. Carnarvon needed an expert and Howard Carter needed a job – it suited them both. His lordship would pay Carter a salary of £400 a year, for which Carter would offer his talents and advice on excavations each season.

Once a year the Commission for Antiquities met and issued licences for digging. A permit to dig a certain area was known as a concession. The chairman of the Commission was Carter's old boss, Gaston Maspero. Carnarvon was impatient for results and found the system frustrating. His choice of what spot he could dig was limited and if the area proved barren he couldn't change his concession until the following season. At times he felt he was treated as a well-meaning amateur. However, now he had Carter to lend his excavations an air of professional know-how, it would improve his standing with Maspero. At first Carnarvon made all the decisions, armed only with a beginner's enthusiasm. He chose the places to dig and hired the foremen. Gradually he learned to respect his expert's greater experience and let Carter take the lead. The two men couldn't have been more different. Lord Carnarvon was wealthy, well travelled and well connected. No doubt he found the younger man rather serious and self-absorbed. While Porchy was good company, with an endless fund of stories, Carter was a loner by nature. His employer soon discovered he could be prickly, even with his friends.

Carnarvon prided himself that he'd learned on his travels to get on with anyone. Yet sometimes he must have wondered if Carter was more at ease with his Egyptian workmen than he was with Europeans. Carter's manners – after years of living alone – were hardly those of a gentleman. Porchy must have winced as Carter picked his hollow tooth with a matchstick after dinner or helped himself to far too much whisky.

For all Carter's faults, Carnarvon grew to like his new companion over the next five years. Beneath the gruff exterior, he found Carter loyal, honest and totally dedicated to his work.

Their second season – under Carter's guidance – was a great success. Carter found the decorated tomb of

Tetiky, an early mayor of Thebes – on the Theban west bank. Other important finds came to light in the following three seasons. Carter and Carnarvon published an account of their early work – *Five Years Exploration at Thebes (1907 – 1911)* – and with it, made their mark in the world of archaeology.

It was a promising start but Carnarvon had set his sights higher. He had ambitions to dig in the Valley of the Kings – where the great Pharaohs of Egypt were buried. Carter inspired Carnarvon with his dream of finding an intact royal tomb. The other royal Valley tombs had been stripped bare in ancient times by grave robbers, but finding an untouched tomb held out the promise of fabulous wealth. Carnarvon – like many before him – was drawn by the lure of buried treasure.

The concession for the Valley of the Kings was held by the American amateur archaeologist, Theodore Davis. It wasn't until 1914 that Davis gave it up, convinced that there were no more tombs to be found in the Valley. (Davis was 77 and died a few months later in February 1915.) Carnarvon eagerly took up the concession, but unfortunately the First World War broke out in 1914, which meant he was stranded in England since travel was too dangerous. In any case in the spring of 1917 he suffered another severe bout of illness. Once again, Carnarvon almost died, saved only by an operation on his septic appendix. Carter, meanwhile, was employed by the British Foreign Office as a diplomatic messenger in Cairo.

By late 1917 the prospects were better with Carnarvon recovering and the war drawing to an end in the Middle East. The plan Carter put to Carnarvon was to make a systematic clearance of the Valley of the Kings. No one had ever attempted such a mammoth task but Carter was sure that places had been missed because they were buried under the rubble of other excavations.

For the next five years – between 1917 and 1922 – Carnarvon employed Carter to work in the Valley each season. Carnarvon's companion was his daughter, Evelyn, a young woman of 20 by 1921. Naturally Evelyn spent a lot of time in Carter's company and the two grew close. Perhaps Porchy occasionally wondered if his daughter was more than fond of Carter. But she was only half his age and a little girlish flirtation was natural. Carter knew where to draw the line; he was always polite and charming with her, nothing more. They exchanged fond letters but the question of marriage would never have arisen as Evelyn and Carter came from vastly different social worlds.

Carnarvon employed a vast team of boys and men, managed by Carter, and they began to clear the land down to the bedrock in the search for a tomb that might have been missed. Thousands of tons of rubble were piled into baskets and taken away by hand-operated railway trucks. Sites that had already been excavated were dug over again in case a tomb entrance had been missed. The results were pitiful. Apart from a few ancient jars, Carnarvon had nothing to show for his expense.

By 1922 Lord Carnarvon felt the time had come to admit defeat. He hated to see waste. He couldn't bear the thought that the money he was paying out season after season was not giving him something in return. To him, excavation was an investment – he put in time and money and expected to see something back. He was the one paying Carter's salary and he was interested in results – things that he could hold in his hand. Dates and inscriptions – the dry bones of history – left Carnarvon cold. He was interested in finding objects of outstanding beauty for his collection. A friend, Wallis Budge of the British Museum, said of Carnarvon:

He only cared for the best, and nothing but the best would satisfy him, and having obtained the best he persisted in believing that there must be something better than the best!

With Carter's help, Carnarvon was building one of the finest private collections of Egyptian art in the world. It was a rich man's market but Carnarvon could afford the prices. Some of the antiques Carter bought in the bazaars were sold on to museums at a profit, but just as many passed into his employer's hands.

But Carnarvon's collection had gained nothing from the Valley of the Kings. Despite Carter's unswerving belief that there was still one more royal tomb, they had drawn a blank. With a heavy heart, Carnarvon sent for Carter. He hated to admit defeat, but there was no sense in throwing good money after bad. He had spent a small fortune and got nothing back. It was obvious that the Valley was exhausted, just as all the experts believed.

Porchy greeted Carter warmly when he arrived, but the awkward subject hung in the air between them. He suspected Carter knew what was on his mind and had come prepared for the worst.

As soon as they were settled in their armchairs, Porchy began to work his way round to breaking the bad news. He reviewed the record of their five years of work in the Valley of the Kings. He took great care to praise all Carter's efforts. No man could have worked harder. But sadly, they were all having to tighten their belts after the war. They'd found nothing and it was time to call a halt to the project.

Carter wasn't ready to give in. He stubbornly clung to his belief that there might be one more tomb in the Valley. The job of clearing the Valley was not yet finished. What if they gave up and missed an untouched royal tomb?

It was the same old familiar tune and Porchy shook his head. He knew Carter's stubborn nature. If he believed in something, nothing would ever convince him he was wrong. Carnarvon's patience was running out. He pointed out that they'd spent five seasons in the same area. There could hardly be a stone in the Valley left unturned. His mind was made up and Carter would just have to accept the situation. It was time to abandon the Valley of the Kings and admit defeat.

A Step in the Rock

1914 – 5 November 1922

THE WAR YEARS had not been wasted for Howard Carter. As a messenger of the King, he was needed to carry secret communications for the British army and occasionally act as a translator in negotiations with Arab contacts. Carter's duties were light since the Middle East was largely in the grip of the Turkish army. He had little to do and a reputation as an awkward customer, which prevented him being employed too often. His duties left him time to tramp through the Valley with a notebook and pick, tapping the rock to see if there was a hollow space underneath.

He believed he'd found clues to Tutankhamun in the discoveries made by Theodore Davis. Davis had found a cup and other fragments bearing the names of Tutankhamun and his queen. Based on these finds, the American claimed that he'd actually found the burial place of the Pharaoh in a small pit tomb. Carter dismissed the claim as *"tommy rot"* – a phrase often heard on his lips when he disagreed. In his opinion all the clues pointed to one thing – Tutankhamun's tomb was still somewhere in the Valley, waiting to be discovered.

Was he wasting his time? Carter knew that everyone else thought so. The Valley had been dug over a hundred times and Theodore Davis was convinced that there were no more tombs to be found there. All the Pharaohs thought to be buried in the Valley had been accounted for apart from three: Smenkhkare, Ramesses VIII and the obscure boy-king called Tutankhamun. Of these, Carter felt Tutankhamun's tomb was the most likely to be found.

Carter would have read everything about Tutankhamun he could find in the years that he spent searching for the elusive tomb. The few details we know are enough to fire the imagination. Tutankhamun was just a boy when he came to the throne of Egypt and was no more than 16 or 17 when he died.

All the clues point to Akhenaten as the boy's father. Akhenaten – known as the "heretic king" (a false believer) – turned his back on Egypt's traditional gods and wanted his subjects to worship only Aten as the One God. Tutankhamun's mother may have been Nefertiti, Akhenaten's beautiful queen, or more likely one of the king's lesser wives, such as the Lady Kiya.

When Akhenaten turned away from Amun-Re, King of

Gods, he moved his capital from Thebes to a site called Tel el Amarna, where he built a new city. But when the heretic king died, everything changed. The worship of Aten had been unpopular and the priests clamoured for a return to their old gods. The court moved back to Thebes and with it Amun-Re and the old religion were re-established.

Tutankhamun came to the throne in about 1333 BC at a time of turmoil in Egypt's history. He was only a young boy of ten years old but was already married to a girl queen, Ankhesenamun – the third daughter of Akhenaten and Nefertiti. It's probable that Tutankhamun married his sister or half-sister, which was normal for Pharaohs. It was one way of keeping the succession in the family.

The young king's hold on his throne was never secure and his short life would have been filled with danger. All Pharaohs were worshipped as gods, but Tutankhamun was only ten and there were older figures around him holding the reins of government. Powerful politicians eyed the throne greedily. His chief adviser, a man called Ay, may have been plotting against him since he had ambitions to become king himself. Tutankhamun and his bride were little more than children. Even worse, they were the children of a hated king. Later, Akhenaten's name would be erased from all his monuments in disgrace. Tutankhamun's reign lasted for only nine years and his death is a mystery.

This much Carter knew about the shadowy monarch he was looking for. But when he received Carnarvon's summons to Highclere Castle in 1922, he knew it could all be for nothing. The whole future of his work in the Valley hung in the balance. He was well aware that his employer's patience was exhausted. The situation looked bleak. He didn't have Carnarvon's great wealth to finance his work, yet he was prepared to gamble everything on his faith in the Valley.

There's no doubt Carter liked and respected his patron. He watched Carnarvon's easy manner with people and learned from him. In some ways Carter tried to model himself on the polished aristocrat, who moved easily in high society. Yet Carter could never forget that it was a master-servant relationship. His salary reminded him of that every month. He didn't have a private fortune behind him and survived on what Carnarvon paid him year by year. Perhaps this dependency gnawed away at his soul over the years. In his three-volume book *The Tomb of Tutankhamun* Carter angrily challenges the popular view of archaeology as an amusing hobby for the rich:

> *Excavation is [thought to be] a sort of super-tourist amusement, carried out with the excavator's own money if he is rich enough, or with other people's money if he can persuade them to subscribe it, and all he has to do is enjoy life in a beautiful winter climate and pay a gang of natives to find things for him. The serious excavator's life is frequently monotonous and ... quite as hard working as that of any other member of society.*

The passage doesn't mention Carnarvon by name, but Carter seems to have had him in mind. Carter certainly regarded himself as a *"serious"* archaeologist, but wouldn't have placed his employer in the same category. Carnarvon kept out of the heat and flies while he watched his men do the work, he rarely got his hands dirty and was often absent when any discovery was made. It was Carter who did all the hard work and he didn't always get the credit. Perhaps this was the worm that ate away inside Carter and would eventually lead to a breakdown in the relationship.

Yet on his way to Highclere in the summer of 1922, Carter wasn't thinking of his grievances. He was thinking of how he could persuade Carnarvon to agree to one more season in the Valley. Knowing he would be hard to convince, Carter had prepared his case. In his pocket he had a map of the Valley of the Kings showing the record of their excavations season by season. At first glance it seemed that they had covered every inch of rock. But Carter had marked in pencil a triangular area close to the entrance to the tomb of Ramesses VI.

When Carnarvon declared it was time to admit defeat, Carter played his final trump card by spreading the map on the table. Not every part of the Valley had been covered, he explained. The map showed one small area they hadn't explored. Twice Carter had put it off for a later date when tourists wouldn't be in the way. Now he felt he couldn't leave the Valley until this triangle of land had been excavated. The area was hidden by some workmen's huts from the time of Ramesses VI. Almost certainly it had been ignored by previous excavations.

Carter sensed that his patron was tempted. He pressed home his advantage, offering to pay the expense of one more season himself if Carnarvon would just allow him to use his concession. It was a deliberate appeal to his patron's sporting nature – one last gamble. And it worked. Carnarvon offered his hand. They would go back for one more season, but it would be at his expense. Who could tell – maybe fortune would finally smile on them?

By 1 November 1922, Carter was back in the Valley of the Kings to begin his search. When it wasn't overrun by tourists, the Valley had a stark beauty of its own. It lies about five kilometres west of Luxor in Upper Egypt – a lonely valley, hemmed in by rocky hills. No river runs through it, there is not even a blade of grass. The landscape is as dry and barren as a desert, and in the early morning the hills turn gold in the sunlight. One peak stands out from the rest, shaped like a pyramid. The Egyptians believed it was the home of the Valley's snake goddess – Meret-seger – which means "lover of silence". Beneath the hills are shadows in the Valley – gaping holes cut into the rock. These are the entrances to the tombs of the mighty Pharaohs, hollowed out over 3,000 years ago. There are more than 80 tombs and burial pits in the Valley. Once they housed the mummified bodies of

Pharaohs such as Ramesses the Great. Some of the graves are hundreds of feet deep with corridors leading from one shadowy chamber to the next. This was the valley where Carter had come looking for the forgotten tomb of Tutankhamun.

Arriving in Cairo, one of Carter's first purchases was a canary bird in a golden cage to keep him company at his house. His servants immediately welcomed the pet as a golden bird that would bring luck. This year, they said, we will find a tomb full of gold.

As Carter started work on a Wednesday morning, he hoped they were right. The task of clearing the area in front of the tomb of Ramesses VI was a mammoth one. There were piles of chippings left by previous excavations. Beneath this rubble lay the ancient workmen's huts Carter had described to Lord Carnarvon. They were rough stone huts probably used by the same workmen who had carved out Ramesses' tomb. It took three days to lay bare the foundation stones of the huts – which lay about a metre above the bedrock floor of the Valley. Once the huts had been noted and cleared away, Carter's men could remove the debris that lay beneath them. What he was searching for was evidence of a staircase leading steeply down below the rock. Such hidden stairways could be seen all around the Valley where they led down into royal tombs.

It was on the fourth morning of November that Carter got the first sign that Tutankhamun was closer than he could have imagined.

As soon as Carter arrived he realized that work had stopped and something out of the ordinary had happened. The headman of his team informed him that something had been found under the very first hut to be cleared. A step cut in the rock. It seemed almost too good to be true. After five years of disappointment, however, Carter didn't let his hopes run away with him, but the signs were promising. As the soil was dug away it became clear that the step was part of a steep cut in the rock some four metres below the entrance to the tomb of Ramesses VI. Even better, it looked like a sunken stairway of the kind used in important tombs. *"I almost dared to hope that we had found our tomb at last,"* said Carter.

Throughout the whole of that day, work continued at a feverish pace. It was not until the next afternoon that the mass of rubble had been cleared away. Now the upper edges of the hidden stairway were visible on all four sides. Carter was convinced that he really had found the entrance to a tomb. Yet still doubts plagued him. How many times had his hopes been raised only to be dashed?

There was always the possibility that the tomb would be unfinished – a grave that was never used. Even if it was finished, it was likely to be empty since tomb robberies were common in ancient Egypt (often those who built the tombs came back to rob them later). Yet there was always the slim chance that this tomb had survived untouched. Carter watched with growing excitement as, one by one, the steps of the staircase were laid bare.

The staircase gradually became a passageway around three metres high and two metres wide – its roof made of rock where it was cut into the hillside. Work progressed more rapidly – with each step leading them down. As daylight began to fade and the sun sank in the sky, Carter finally saw what he'd been looking for. At the level of the twelfth step there was the upper part of a doorway – blocked, plastered and sealed up.

It was a moment worth five years of toil. *"I think my first feeling was one of congratulation that my faith in the Valley had not been unjustified,"* Carter said later. *"With excitement growing to fever heat I searched the seal for evidence of the owner, but could find no name."*

What he did find was a seal stamped in the plaster showing the jackal-god Anubis – divine protector of the grave. At the god's feet, nine bound prisoners represented the enemies of Egypt. This royal seal told Carter that the tomb belonged to someone of real importance – if not a Pharaoh then certainly a high-ranking noble. What's more, the sealed door was hidden under the workmen's huts built in the time of Ramesses VI, which showed that it hadn't been entered after that date. If it had stayed hidden for so long then maybe it hadn't been robbed like most of the tombs in the Valley. It was a thrilling moment. The moment Carter had been waiting for half his life. For now he remained in the dark – not yet knowing, but daring to hope…

Alone save for my native workmen, I found myself ... on the threshold of what might prove to be a magnificent discovery. Anything, literally anything might lie beyond that passage, and it needed all my self-control to keep from breaking down the doorway, and investigating then and there.

One thing puzzled Carter. The opening was small compared to the other Valley tombs. Was it only the tomb of a noble? Or was it just a hidden store for royal possessions? Carter hoped not. He desperately wanted to believe that he was looking at the doorway to Tutankhamun's final resting-place.

While he was examining the seal he noticed some of the plaster had fallen away at the top of the door. Unable to contain his impatience, Carter took a chisel and chipped away at the hole until it was big enough to insert an electric torch. What he could see inside would have disappointed most people – it was a passageway filled from floor to ceiling with stone and rubble. But Carter viewed it with satisfaction – the doorways to important tombs were often blocked up with rubble to make it harder for thieves to break in. It proved that he was dealing with a tomb of real importance.

It was late – the moon had stolen into the sky and Carter reluctantly had to admit that nothing more could be done that day. A few centimetres further down the door, he would have found another seal, revealing the name of the tomb's owner. Had he known he could have saved himself many sleepless nights. But it was dark – and Carter had to control his impatience. Much as he wanted to push ahead with clearing the passageway the next day – he would have to wait. Carter was not his own master. His arrangement with Lord Carnarvon obliged him to wait for his patron's arrival before going any further. Carter records this decision in his diary matter-of-factly, but it must have taken all his self-control to make it. There would be weeks of waiting before Lord Carnarvon could arrive. Meanwhile he had to live with the agony of not knowing precisely what he'd found. All the signs were good – but they were only signs. Was this to be another disappointment or had he, at last, found the royal tomb he was looking for?

These were the questions occupying Carter as he rode his mule home along the ghostly moonlit Valley. Behind him lay the tomb with its secrets still untold. Carter had filled in the staircase with loose rubble and posted his most trustworthy workmen to guard the tomb for the night. Modern Egypt was no different from ancient times – tomb robbers were a constant danger. The next morning he would send off a telegram to his employer telling him of the wonderful discovery. Until Carnarvon arrived there was nothing to do but wait.

Carnarvon
"Wonderful Things"
6 – 26 November 1922

LORD CARNARVON READ the telegram again.

6TH NOVEMBER 1922 – LUXOR

AT LAST HAVE MADE WONDERFUL DISCOVERY
IN VALLEY – A MAGNIFICENT TOMB WITH SEALS
INTACT – RECOVERED SAME FOR YOUR ARRIVAL
– CONGRATULATIONS – CARTER.

It was stunning news. Carnarvon hadn't honestly expected Carter to find anything in the Valley. In fact he had only agreed to another season out of respect for his friend's determination. From his point of view the last five years had been disappointing. At the burial site in Thebes they had found a number of important tombs and temples but from the moment they switched to the

Valley the well had run dry. Carnarvon was as keen to find the lost tomb of Tutankhamun as Carter, but he'd begun to doubt if it really existed.

Now came this telegram just four days after Carter started work in the Valley. It promised a *"magnificent tomb"*. But whose tomb was it? Carter's telegram didn't say – either because he didn't know or because he expected Carnarvon to guess. Was it meant to be a coded message meaning that Carter had actually found Tutankhamun? And if the seals were intact could it mean they'd found what they were seeking? The tomb of a Pharaoh, intact, with all the king's priceless possessions buried with him ready for his journey into the next world. Carnarvon's mind reeled at the possibilities. What would they find behind the door? He had already built one of the best private collections of Egyptian art in the world – most of the pieces picked out by Carter's shrewd eye in Egyptian bazaars. But to enter the tomb of an actual Pharaoh and hold those treasures in his hand, what a moment that would be!

Carnarvon replied to Carter's telegram by return: *"Possibly come soon."* By the next day he had made his arrangements. Carnarvon travelled out with his daughter, Evelyn, to keep him company. They stepped off the train at Luxor on 23 November. By the next afternoon Carter and his team had cleared away the rubble to reveal 16 steps in all. The door that Carter had examined before was now revealed from top to bottom. Carnarvon was able to see for himself the seal in the plaster with the jackal and nine captives. More importantly, he was able to examine other seals nearer the base – which hadn't been visible to Carter before. Carnarvon crouched down beside Carter as he examined them.

The name they found on the seals was Tutankhamun.

It was almost too good to be true. Carnarvon and his partner were speechless for a moment, overcome by relief and delight. Yet, almost as soon as their hopes were raised, they were dashed again.

It was Carter who saw it first. Without a word he pointed to the upper right-hand side of the doorway. Carnarvon saw the patch – about half a metre in diameter – where the wall had plainly been replastered twice. The untouched part of the doorway bore the seal of Tutankhamun, while the replastered portions carried the royal seal of the jackal and nine captives.

Carnarvon was no expert but he knew what a closed up hole meant. Robbers had entered before them – perhaps more than once. The door had evidently been re-sealed at a later date. Still, if someone had taken the trouble to seal the door carefully, didn't that suggest something worth protecting remained inside? If the tomb had been robbed, maybe it wasn't completely empty. Carnarvon's senses were reeling. One moment he felt dizzy with success, the next he was teetering on the edge of despair.

The puzzle grew more confusing still. Who was the owner of the tomb? As the workmen began to clear the rubble that filled the staircase they came across broken pots, clay seals and boxes. These bore the names of different Pharaohs from various dates – Akhenaten, Amenhetep II, as well as Tutankhamun. There was a green *scarab* – a carved beetle – of the Pharaoh Tuthmosis III. Carnarvon was baffled by this confusing mixture of names. Not until they got beyond the sealed door and the rubble on the other side would they have the answer to the riddle.

Carnarvon had arrived with high hopes, but now the picture was unclear. The puzzling evidence seemed to point to a collection of random objects from different dates that had been buried in a hiding place. For the moment, Tutankhamun's tomb seemed as far away as it had ever been.

Next morning they began to remove the large stones that blocked up the inner door. Behind it, they found a passageway about two metres high that led downwards. It was filled from floor to ceiling with rubble as Carter had seen earlier.

Further evidence of the robbers' entry was here. The rubble was of a darker colour in the upper left-hand corner, where the robbers' tunnel had been filled in. Empty waterskins and broken pots also showed the plunderers had passed this way. Yet Carter pointed out that it would have been difficult to remove anything large through so small a tunnel.

All day the clearing went on, moving forwards painfully slowly. Carnarvon knew that excavation couldn't be hurried, nevertheless it must have tried his patience. His health was too fragile for him to lend a hand in any of the heavy work. He remained a helpless bystander for hour after hour, which didn't make the waiting any easier. What lay ahead at the end of this corridor? Were they nearing their goal at last?

Morning dawned on 26 November – a day that Carnarvon would remember for the rest of his life. All morning the work of clearing the passageway went on, revealing delicate fragments of painted vases and alabaster jars mixed in with the chips of rubble. About three o' clock in the afternoon Carnarvon was able to see it – a second inner door almost an exact copy of the first – nine metres from the entrance.

This doorway also showed evidence of a hole plastered over – but it was so small it was difficult to believe any man could have squeezed through. The seals again clearly showed the signs of a royal burial site and Tutankhamun.

Slowly, far too slowly for Carnarvon's nerves, the passage was cleared until the doorway was visible from top to bottom. The moment had arrived. It was now three weeks since the first step in the sand had been discovered. The answers to Carnarvon's questions, the confirmation of his highest hopes or his worst fears, surely lay beyond this door. He was burning to see inside for himself but felt the privilege rightly lay with Carter. Trying to sound calm he asked Carter to make a gap in the plaster so he could look in.

He watched Carter chisel a small hole at the upper left-hand corner of the door. When it was done Carter slid an iron testing rod through the hole to see if it met any resistance. He nodded to show the rod had found nothing but darkness and hollow space. The space behind the door wasn't blocked by more rubble. Next Carter lit a candle and held it up to the hole to test for poisonous gases. The flame flickered in the hot air but stayed alight. Carnarvon watched Carter enlarge the hole further to make it large enough to push the candle inside. No doubt he had to resist the impulse to grab the chisel from his partner's hand and do the job faster himself. Behind him stood his daughter, Evelyn, watching eagerly. For the last few minutes they had hardly spoken a word.

At last Carter was able to push his hand through the hole. Standing behind him, Carnarvon's nerves were drawn as tight as a bowstring. The silence seemed to go on for ever. Longer than he could bear.

"Well? What is it? Can you see anything?" he asked in a voice that trembled.

"Yes," replied Carter. *"Wonderful things."*

The Day of Days

7 – 26 November 1922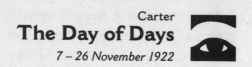

THE LAST TWO WEEKS had been the longest of Howard Carter's life. Since sending off the telegram to Carnarvon he had not been idle. News travelled fast in Egypt and no discovery could be kept a secret for long. Carter received a steady stream of congratulations and offers of help from every quarter.

Most of these he ignored, but he already felt the job was too big for him alone.

Carnarvon wouldn't be much help in the hard work of clearing a way to the tomb. His employer would potter around as usual, asking questions and making suggestions in his interested fashion. Carter needed a younger and fitter man to help him. He sent a telegram to Arthur Callender inviting him to join the work. Callender was a trained architect and engineer whose previous jobs included manager of the Egyptian branch railway. He'd acted as Carter's assistant on other digs and was well used to the excavator's quick temper.

Callender had come promptly and spent a day clearing away the upper layer of rubbish. By the time Carnarvon arrived everything was ready to start work on the stairway. The early signs had been puzzling and disturbing. Carter had been bitterly disappointed by the evidence that robbers had broken into the tomb. Then his hopes had risen again when they uncovered the second door with the seal clear as day: Tutankhamun.

Finally he was ready to insert a candle into the hole he'd made at the corner of the door. What had he expected to see as he craned his head forward and peered into the void beyond? A second staircase? An empty chamber? He had no idea. But nothing could have prepared him for what lay inside that dark vault beneath the rock.

As his eyes slowly began to adjust to the inky darkness of the chamber, he forgot everything except his curiosity. Even the impatience of Carnarvon at his shoulder was forgotten. Nothing else existed except this time, this place and the mystery that lay before him. The candle flickered as hot air trapped inside the chamber escaped, making shadows leap and dance. He found himself looking down into a room sunk about half a metre below the level of the passageway where he was standing. There were shapes down there in the darkness, but as yet they were hard to identify. Carter moved the candle down, casting its light round the chamber.

All at once monstrous beasts seemed to stare back at him. After a moment, he realized they were not real animals but golden couches, carved with the heads of strange beasts. Seen in the candlelight they threw distorted shadows upon the wall and looked startlingly life-like. Carter gazed as if in a trance: *"Details of the room emerged slowly from the mist, strange animals, statues and gold – everywhere the glint of gold."* It was only when Carnarvon spoke that Carter remembered his companions were still waiting anxiously for his verdict.

When he'd made way for Carnarvon to have a brief look, they widened the spy-hole further so that he could insert an electric torch. It was only at this point that Carter began to grasp the scale of their find. What they were looking at was not just a few objects; it was a treasure house, a cave of wonders. The entire room (later known as the antechamber) was crammed to the ceiling with priceless relics of every kind.

In one corner was a confused pile of wheels and shapes that the torch beam revealed as overturned chariots. From behind them peered the portrait of an ancient king. From the open door of a black shrine the head of a great golden snake emerged as if it were about to uncoil and slide on to the floor. Everywhere there were caskets, vases, beds and beautifully carved chairs. There were boxes of all shapes and designs, and bouquets of leaves and flowers preserved astonishingly through the centuries. Most astounding of all were two statues of a Pharaoh, carved in black, wearing gold kilts and gold sandals with the sacred cobra on their foreheads. These two life-size figures faced each other as if keeping guard on the treasures of the chamber.

All his life Carter had dreamed of making a discovery like this. Now the moment had come, he felt as if he was trespassing on holy ground. He had entered tombs and temples before but this time he felt like an intruder. Time seemed to have stood still in this sacred place.

Three thousand, four thousand years maybe, have passed and gone since human feet last trod the floor on which you stand and yet, as you note the signs of recent life around you ... you feel it might have been but yesterday. The very air you breathe, unchanged throughout the centuries, you share with those who laid the mummy to rest.

For the rest of his days Carter would never forget that first sight. Surely no one had ever seen anything as breathtaking. The effect was bewildering, overwhelming. Whatever Carter had hoped for, this exceeded it. There was a whole museumful of priceless objects crammed into this one small chamber. Some objects Carter recognized but others were strange and unfamiliar. Most striking of all was the way in which the treasures were piled one on top of another as if they were in a junkyard.

For a long time Carter and his partner gazed in awe-struck silence, unable to take in the meaning of their discovery. Then enlarging the hole further, Carter scrambled through, followed by his three companions.

Slowly, with great care, they picked their way among the heaps of treasure, unable to take it all in.

The three golden couches with the heads of animals revealed another surprise. Crawling underneath and shining his torch, Carter found another sealed door torn open by a jagged robber's hole. Through it he could see another smaller annexe room, if anything even more crammed with objects. The contents were jumbled together in a way that was beyond belief. In the first room there had evidently been some attempt to tidy up after the robbers, but in this room everything was just as the intruders had left it. Hundreds of objects – wine jars, pots, baskets of fruit, boxes stools, chairs and bedsteads – were piled together at random.

As Carter gazed, he was struck by a new, alarming thought. If this really was a Pharaoh's tomb then something was missing from the marvels they had seen. There was no coffin or trace of a mummy. Had they found Tutankhamun or not?

At the far end of the antechamber, between the two statues of a king, Carter found a clue to the mystery. The two black statues of a Pharaoh were not guarding the room at all; they were sentries posted on either side of another sealed door. At the bottom of the door, there was a small hole that had been replastered, evidence that the robbers had entered the next chamber, too.

It gradually dawned on Carter that they were only on the threshold of their discovery. For all its treasures, the room he was looking at was only an entrance room!

Behind that sealed door there might be other chambers, possibly a whole series of them. And in one of those rooms Tutankhamun could be waiting for them in his grave.

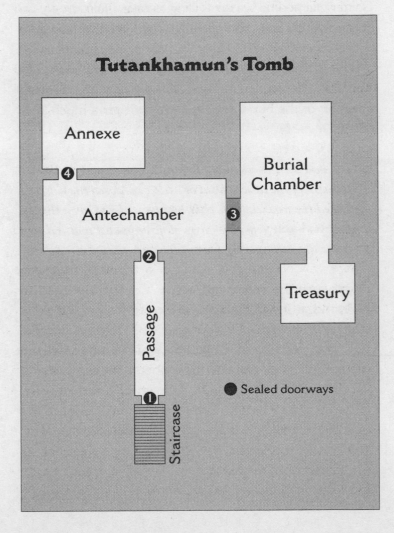

"*Our natural impulse,*" admitted Carter, "*was to break down the door, and get to the bottom of the matter at once, but to do so would have entailed serious risk of damage to many of the objects in the antechamber.*" It was a risk Carter claimed he wasn't willing to take. "*Reluctantly we decided to abandon the opening of this inner sealed door until we had cleared the antechamber of all its contents.*"

This is the account that appears in Carter's book, *The Tomb of Tutankhamun*. The author says the burning question of the burial chamber was left for a much later date.

> *We had seen enough, our brains began to reel at the thought of the task in front of us. We re-closed the hole, locked the wooden grille that had been placed upon the first doorway, left our native staff on guard and rode home down the Valley, strangely silent and subdued.*

This was the version of events Carter presented to the world. But was he hiding a secret?

The Secret

AS THEY RODE HOME down the Valley on their mules, Lord Carnarvon's mind was racing. They had seen so many marvels that day he could hardly make sense of them. The morning had started with the painfully slow work of clearing the remaining rubble from the passageway. At that point he'd tried to prepare himself for disappointment. Then they had reached the second door and he had got his first thrilling glimpse of gold by the light of the candle. When they'd finally scrambled into the chamber, it had been beyond anything he could ever have imagined. He tried to recall small details, such as the golden throne of the king – with a scene of the Pharaoh and his queen, made entirely from semi-precious stones. The beauty of the work was breathtaking. Yet his mind kept returning to something else – the sealed door between the two immense statues.

Like Carter, he had noticed the clear outline of the robber's hole. It was now sealed up but once it had been big enough for a small person to crawl through. Someone as thin as him for example.

Neither he nor Carter had yet voiced what must have crossed both their minds. Here was a way into the burial chamber that was surely on the other side of the wall. The hole offered them a chance to find out once and for all whether Tutankhamun was there. In Carnarvon's view it was an invitation they couldn't turn down. He was too impatient to wait weeks or even months. They didn't have to break down the entire wall. Instead they could easily re-open the robber's hole and crawl through, just to take a look. What could be simpler? The hole had been opened once by the tomb robbers, so why couldn't it be opened again? But would Carter agree? Surely he felt the same fever to know what lay beyond that wall?

Carnarvon's desire to know what was in the burial chamber was perfectly reasonable, but Carter may have pointed out the problems. Playing it by the book, they should wait to make a record of what was in the first room (the antechamber), before they touched anything at all. Tunnelling through a wall posed a risk that something might get damaged. Strictly speaking, the Department of Antiquities should also be informed before they went any further. The Department would expect to be present when the burial chamber was opened and Carter as an ex-inspector himself, would have been well aware of this.

Furthermore, if the existence of the robber's hole became known, every tourist and official in Egypt would want to crawl through and get a glimpse of the burial chamber. The word would spread like wildfire. It would be impossible for Carter to start the delicate work of clearing the first chamber under such circumstances.

Yet the fact remained, if they waited until they could clear the antechamber, there would be a delay of weeks, even months. It didn't bear thinking about.

The solution the two men agreed on was to keep the robber's hole a secret. No one was to know of their plan. They would enter through the hole at night and plaster it over again afterwards.

None of Carnarvon's letters or articles mention breaking into the burial chamber. Neither did the account Carter published later. The whole episode remained a closely kept secret long after the event, at first known only to Carnarvon, his daughter, Carter, Callender and a few loyal guards. Later the truth leaked out to a few others.

Carnarvon probably had his own reasons for keeping the entry into the burial chamber a secret. If he was already considering selling the story to the newspapers, it would be useful to keep the public waiting in breathless suspense for a little longer. Much better to have a drama about to unfold than one that had already taken place.

The secret only became known months later. Carnarvon's half-brother, Mervyn Herbert heard it on the day of the official opening of the burial chamber.

Evelyn had been told by her father to let him in on the secret.

> *This she did under the promise of the strictest secrecy.*
> *It is a thing I would never give away in any case, and it*
> *is one which I think ought not to be known, at any rate,*
> *not at the present. Here is the secret. They had both*
> *been into the second chamber! After the discovery they*
> *had not been able to resist it – they had made a small*
> *hole in the wall (which they afterwards filled up again)*
> *and climbed through. She described to me very shortly*
> *some of the extraordinary wonders I was about to see.*

Alfred Lucas, a chemist who later joined the team, learned the secret from Carter's lips. Soon after he started work, Carter pointed out the plastered-over robber's hole. (In photographs of the sealed door, the robber's hole is covered by a cleverly placed basket lid and some reeds.) Carter had said that the hole had been re-sealed in ancient times after the tomb robbers. This was true but when Lucas remarked that it didn't look like old plasterwork, Carter admitted it wasn't. He'd re-opened the robber's hole and then plastered over it himself.

Which night they went in, we don't know for sure, but it must have been before 27 November when the antechamber was officially opened. It's easy enough to imagine the details. Late one night, under the cover of darkness, Carnarvon and Evelyn would have made their way down the ghostly valley to the tomb. Perhaps they met Carter and Callender at the tomb that night, since the pair sometimes slept there for added security. Guards would have been posted at the tomb's entrance. These were Carnarvon's own trusted men. No doubt he gave strict orders that no one else was to be allowed in, while the four of them went down into the tomb.

Shining their electric torches they unlocked the metal grille and entered. They picked their way past the precious relics strewn around the floor of the antechamber. Their torch beams illuminated the robber's hole, which could be seen plainly at the bottom of the sealed doorway. It was just big enough for a small person to wriggle through. Carnarvon must have felt confident of getting through since poor health had left him matchstick thin. Evelyn was equally slim for fashionable reasons. Carter was more bulky and the fourth member of the group, Callender, found he was too big to squeeze through.

The lateness of the hour and the two brooding shadows of the black statues lent the scene an eerie stillness. What passed through Carnarvon's mind as Carter carefully chipped away at the plaster? He must have felt like one of the ancient tomb robbers, breaking into the last resting-place of the god-like Pharaoh. Secrecy and darkness added to the air of excitement. In the next few minutes he would know for certain whether the mummified body of Tutankhamun lay on the other side of that wall.

Finally the sound of Carter's hammer and chisel ceased. The hole was ready. One by one Carter, Carnarvon and Evelyn crawled through the jagged gap.

Once on the other side, they stood upright to find themselves in a surprisingly small chamber. There was hardly any room to move because something large and box-shaped filled the space. It was cold to the touch. When Carnarvon shone his torch, the stone shone as if it was made of solid gold. He was looking at the burial shrine of Tutankhamun.

Carter
The Shadowy King
26 November – 4 December 1922

CARTER HAD HIS OWN REASONS for making sure that the boy-king really was inside the tomb. They were based on bitter experience. Many years before, as a young archaeological inspector, he had opened another tomb with high hopes, and he could still remember the burning humiliation of that day.

The tomb was known as el Bab-el-Hosan (tomb of the horse) because Carter's horse was the one to find it. One day in November 1898, when he had been out riding near Deir el-Bahri, his horse stumbled in a crater in the sand. Carter immediately suspected he might have found a hidden tomb.

Scraping away the sand, he found stonework that confirmed his hopes. Two months of work then revealed a doorway sealed up with mud bricks. Confident that he was about to uncover something spectacular, the young inspector had invited the British Consul, Lord Cromer, to witness the opening of the tomb. But Carter was too eager to show off his success. Inside he found nothing but a large sandstone statue of a king and an empty coffin. The life-size statue of the king Mentuhotep had been laid to rest in its grave just like a human body. It had been a remarkable find but to Carter it only represented a crushing failure. By inviting Lord Cromer to witness his triumph he felt he had made a fool of himself.

It had been a bitter disappointment and one that Carter never forgot. So when Carnarvon offered Carter the chance to enter Tutankhamun's burial chamber, he couldn't resist. This time he would make *certain* before announcing the news to the world.

That night in the Valley of the Kings was the crowning moment of Carter's career. He had found tombs before, but he had never looked on the intact shrine of a king in all its splendour. Other men dream of fame, riches or power. Howard Carter dreamed of finding a mummy in its royal tomb. This was his finest hour.

Carter knew that the robbers had penetrated as far as the burial chamber. It was all too possible that the thieves had opened the king's grave and plundered what was inside. But once Carter stood before the shrine and shone his torch on its massive shape he must have felt a huge wave of relief. His triumph was complete. All the signs were that the shrine was unharmed. "*I have got*

Tutankhamun (that is certain) and I believe intact," Carter wrote in a letter.

Evelyn later wrote to thank Carter for allowing her to be one of the three people in the world to enter that sacred place. *"It was the* Great Moment *of my life,"* she said. No doubt Carter agreed. This was the fulfilment of everything he'd worked for since the age of 17. Nothing that came afterwards would be as pure or wonderful as that moment. He, Howard Carter, the son of a poor Norfolk artist, had seen what other archaeologists could only dream of.

By the morning of the 27 November (probably just after the secret entry) Carter was ready to start work officially in the antechamber. Once the outer door was unblocked, Carter could survey the antechamber with the aid of electric lights connected to the main Valley power supply. The size of the task would have daunted anyone. Clearing the first room alone would take weeks, months of work. *"The thing was outside all experience, bewildering and for the moment it seemed as though there were more to be done than any human agency could accomplish,"* wrote Carter.

As he examined the incredible jumble, he tried to piece together the evidence like a detective surveying the scene of a crime. What had happened in this dark chamber 3,000 years before?

The mystery puzzling Carter was the unfinished robbery. Why wasn't Tutankhamun's tomb stripped bare in ancient times like the other tombs in the Valley of the Kings?

The robbers had certainly had the chance. Everywhere their handiwork could be seen. Objects lay overturned and heaped together in piles. Some of the gold struts of the Pharaoh's throne had been broken off. Carter found a handful of solid gold rings knotted in a piece of linen and then abandoned in a box. At the back of the antechamber, under the golden couches, they had found an annexe room – smaller than the burial chamber. Here there was even more confusion. Carter wrote:

> *One [robber] – there would probably not have been room for more than one – had crept into the chamber, and had then hastily but systematically ransacked its entire contents, emptying boxes, throwing things aside, piling them one upon another, and occasionally passing objects through the hole to his companions for closer examination in the outer chamber. He had done his work just about as thoroughly as an earthquake.*

Carter concluded there must have been two separate robberies, both attempted soon after Tutankhamun's burial. He found the thieves had looted cosmetics, which wouldn't have lasted long in Egypt's hot climate – that seemed to rule out a robbery much later. The door to the tomb looked as if it had been closed and re-sealed twice, which supported the theory of two robberies. The first robbers seemed to have had linen, cosmetics and precious metal on their shopping list. The evidence suggested the second robbery was on a larger scale and that guards or priests had hurriedly tidied up after the thieves. He guessed that the robbers would have ignored the larger items in the chamber since they were too big to carry. Their main interest would have been small items of jewellery, gold or other precious metal. Yet they'd left behind a huge amount that could have been carried. Why, wondered Carter, had they left the job half finished?

He tried to picture the grim details of the story as it might have unfolded. The second set of robbers made a hole in the outer door and tunnelled their way through the blocked passageway. (He estimated it would have taken them seven or eight hours to tunnel through, with a chain of men passing back baskets of rubble.) Breaking through the second doorway, the robbers then found themselves in the dark chamber where Carter was standing. It's easy to imagine their astonishment as they surveyed the golden treasures before them. Greed and wonder mingled with fear. By entering the sacred tomb of a Pharaoh they were risking certain death.

In a fever they began to open box after box, spilling the contents on the floor in their haste. One man found the gold rings and twisted them into a piece of royal linen for safekeeping. Another of the robbers tore a small golden statue from its pedestal. A third snapped off the valuable metal arrowheads and broke off the struts in the Pharaoh's golden throne. In the dark perhaps they blundered around, arguing about what was worth taking and what should be left behind.

And then something went wrong. Maybe they heard shouts of warning from their friends keeping watch at the entrance to the tunnel.

Were they caught in the tomb by the royal guards? Or did they manage to escape in a panic, grabbing whatever they could and dropping part of their plunder, including the bundle of rings? They had certainly left a host of precious items that could have been carried, so one way or another it looked like the robbery was a botched job.

Some objects were missing, however, which suggested that some of the robbers got away. As they tried to flee the scene, their way must have been blocked by one of the animal-shaped couches. Carter found it thrown carelessly on top of another couch, speared on the horns of a cow's head. Probably the unlucky thieves were trapped in the tomb by the guards and faced a terrible punishment for their crime. Robbers were impaled on a sharpened stake and left in the sun to die a slow and painful death.

The officials who re-sealed the tomb seemed to have been in as much of a hurry as the thieves. They re-packed what was left, jamming items into boxes without much thought or care. (In one box for instance, the label still attached stated it contained 17 blue vases. Inside Carter found 16 vases, an ivory casket, a wine strainer, a piece of royal clothing and two throwing sticks used for hunting.) Then the holes into the burial chamber and the antechamber were closed up, plastered over and stamped with the royal seal of the jackal and nine captives.

The passageway was packed again with rubble and the outer door re-sealed. The shadowy tomb was silent once again. There it lay, forgotten for 3,000 years, until Howard Carter's persistence had uncovered it.

In the crowded annexe room, Carter found a white painted box containing the king's hunting bows. On the box could still be seen the dirty footprints of the robbers who had climbed over it. How grateful Carter felt that those robbers hadn't succeeded in stripping the tomb bare!

Now the real work of clearing the first chamber could begin. Carter had two months' work ahead of him; two months of nerve-racking work in a room no bigger than eight metres by five metres and crammed to the ceiling with 600 priceless objects. He compared his delicate task to a *"giant game of spillikins"* – the game where players try to remove one wooden stick without disturbing the rest of the pile.

The first full report on the Tutankhamun story appeared in *The Times* on the 30 November. Arthur Merton, *The Times* chief reporter had arrived for the opening of the tomb the day before and got his information from Carter. That report spread the story like wildfire around the world. By 4 December Carter was ready to invite Merton to his house for a personal interview. In the article he confidently predicted that they would find Tutankhamun in his burial chamber (taking care not to mention *why* he was so confident).

The discovery of the tomb had given Howard Carter a new self-confidence. No longer was he just a failed ex-Inspector of Antiquities – now he was the man who had found Tutankhamun's tomb. Fame had come knocking for Howard Carter … but before long he would be wishing he hadn't opened the door.

Swimming with Sharks
4 December 1922 – 19 January 1923

BY 4 DECEMBER Lord Carnarvon was on his way back to England. The patient work of preserving and recording the objects in the antechamber held no appeal for Carnarvon. He had other weighty matters on his mind. In England he would be the guest of royalty. King George V and Queen Mary were *"most interested"* to learn more about his great discovery. Porchy was also looking forward to seeing his old friend, Alan Gardiner, and persuading the expert of ancient languages to come out to Egypt and lend his help. Above all, the question he turned over and over in his mind was how to deal with the newspapers.

It was clear to Carnarvon from the start that the find was news. Yet he had no idea how Tutankhamun mania would grip the world during the following year. The story had everything – a search for a forgotten king, two heroic adventurers, and most of all the discovery of fabulous gold. Add to this the promise of the mummy in its coffin and it's easy to see how it became the longest-running newspaper story in history.

Carter's interview on 4 December had only further inflamed interest. The thirst for news of the greatest discovery of the century was unquenchable. Something had to be done and Carnarvon realized he had an opportunity to make a lot of money. Any newspaper in the world would pay for the story he had to tell. Better still, it was a story that would keep running for months to come. Carnarvon must have discussed the idea with Carter, who probably didn't share his employer's enthusiasm for selling the story. Carter always felt there was something *unhealthy* in the curiosity of the press. As far as he was concerned, the find was a matter for archaeologists and newspaper talk of *"gold and treasure"* only irritated him.

However, Carnarvon was the one financing the excavation and took a more practical view. The newspapers offered a chance to repay some of his costs – and he knew the expense would run into thousands.

As Carnarvon saw it there were two questions to consider. Firstly, what kind of arrangement would be workable? Secondly, how could he "do the right thing"? It's a phrase that sums up Carnarvon. In many ways honour and decency mattered more to him than profit.

It was an extraordinary position to be in, and one that presented the kind of problem he wasn't used to. As he wrote to Carter, *"Neither of us having much experience of*

press sharks, one is rather at a loss how to act for the best."
The sharks were circling already and the well-meaning
Porchy was easy prey.

Over lunch in his London townhouse in Seamore Place,
Carnarvon discussed the matter with Alan Gardiner.
From the moment of his return to London, every
newspaper in the world wanted to talk to him. Something
would have to be done and the sooner the better.

As if on cue, the phone rang. It was Geoffrey Dawson,
editor of *The Times*. He wanted to come and see
Carnarvon with a proposal. Carnarvon invited him round
on the spot. He wanted to get this business settled so
that the press would leave him alone.

Dawson arrived within the hour. After a little polite
chit-chat, he came straight to the point. He wanted
Carnarvon to give *The Times* exclusive rights to the
Tutankhamun story.

Carnarvon knew that exclusive meant he couldn't sell his
story to anyone else. Would that be in his best interests?

Dawson made a persuasive case. Every newspaper from
New York to Calcutta wanted the story and Carnarvon
would be pestered continuously. He couldn't possibly grant
interviews to everyone. Far better to make *The Times* his
sole agent. That way he would only have to talk to one
reporter. *The Times* would sell the news and pictures to
every other paper in the world, saving Carnarvon the time
and trouble. Dawson claimed his newspaper had reached
a similar agreement with the Royal Geographical Society
to cover an expedition to conquer Mount Everest.

The advantages seemed obvious to Carnarvon. He imagined Carter was in for a difficult time with the press pack descending on the Valley. Didn't it make sense to channel all the information through one newspaper? In practical terms it would save them having to deal with the rival claims of many different reporters. What's more, it would guarantee Carnarvon a large sum of money, without a lot of smaller deals. The question remained, was it a fair arrangement? Fairness mattered to Carnarvon and he wanted to act honourably.

Soon after Dawson's offer, Carnarvon visited the Royal Geographical Society. The secretary assured him their arrangement had been a great success. Yes, some of the papers had grumbled about it, but there was no doubt the deal had worked to their advantage. Carnarvon didn't stop to consider that the two situations couldn't be compared. Mount Everest was hardly swarming with reporters in the same way as the Valley of the Kings.

Just before Christmas, Alan Gardiner journeyed to Egypt, carrying a long letter from Carnarvon to Howard Carter. In it Carnarvon outlined what had happened in the last few weeks and touched on the question of *The Times* agreement. He was, he said, still thinking it over. There was even the possibility of a film to be made of the Tutankhamun discovery. *"There is, I imagine, a good deal of money in this, what I don't know – possibly 10–20 thousand – but there are difficulties,"* he wrote. Referring to *The Times* deal, he said that the Royal Geographical

Society received £1,000 for 15 long reports sent by cable. "*I think the* Daily Mail *would give more, but* The Times *is after all the first newspaper in the world.*"

Two weeks later, on 9 January 1923, Carnarvon had made up his mind and signed the exclusive deal with *The Times*. He wrote to Carter the next day, telling him of his decision. Any less tight an arrangement "*would make the matter too common and commercial*" he argued. Carnarvon's logic is hard to understand, but *The Times* certainly got everything they wanted. In the contract, Carnarvon agreed that neither he nor his staff would offer "*news articles, interviews or photographs*" to anyone besides *The Times*. Even Carnarvon's friends or acquaintances could give no interviews or information to members of the press. *The Times* reporter would accompany Carter's team in the Valley and the London paper would have a monopoly on news. Any paper or magazine in the world who wanted first-hand information would have to negotiate a price with *The Times* editor.

Carnarvon probably felt he'd solved the whole tricky business with one stroke of a pen. If so, he was badly mistaken. *The Times* agreement would turn out to be the biggest blunder he ever made. What's more, the person who stood to suffer most had hardly been consulted. Howard Carter was thousands of miles away in the Valley of the Kings. He had little idea of the storm clouds gathering around him.

Carter
Tutmania!
9 January – 15 February 1923

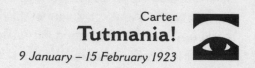

WE CAN ONLY GUESS what Carter thought of his patron's agreement with *The Times*. In public, Carter had to support the decision. After all he was still on Carnarvon's payroll, he could hardly go round publicly criticizing his patron's decisions. Yet in private, Carter must have cursed Carnarvon's blunder a thousand times. Although Carnarvon had kept him informed by letter, his opinion had hardly been consulted. *He* did not stand to make money from the deal. But it was he who suffered the press swarming round the Valley like a plague of locusts. At the time, Carter was too busy with his work to give the newspaper question much attention. It was Carnarvon who was in England and *The Times* deal was his decision. Only in the months to come did Carter begin to grasp the full implications of Carnarvon's mistake.

The Times deal didn't stop every major newspaper from sending their reporter to the Valley. Before long the scene at the tomb began to resemble a high street on carnival day. On 25 January 1923, the *Daily Telegraph* reported:

> The road leading to the rock enclosed ravine ... was packed with vehicles and animals of, every conceivable variety. The guides, donkey boys, sellers of antiquities, and hawkers of lemonade were doing a roaring trade... When the last articles had been removed from the corridor today the newspaper correspondents began a spirited dash across the desert to the banks of the Nile upon donkeys, horses, camels and chariot-like sand carts in a race to be the first to reach the telegraph offices.

Carnarvon's agreement with *The Times* was greeted as an outrage. The other papers simply refused to pay *The Times* for a story they believed was public property. In Luxor the small army of foreign reporters soon joined forces, declaring war on *The Times*. They offered bribes to anyone who could offer inside information on the tomb, including Carter's staff and Egyptian workmen. The press-men interfered with Carter's work and played on his nerves. Carter himself kept a brooding silence but luckily his assistant, Arthur Mace, kept a diary. Mace, an Egyptologist at New York's Metropolitan Museum, was one of Carter's most loyal supporters and his diary captures the tense atmosphere in the camp:

> *26th Jan*
> *The atmosphere of Luxor is nerve-racking at present...*
> *No one talks of anything but the tomb, newspapermen*
> *swarm, and you daren't say a word without looking*
> *around everywhere to see if anyone is listening...*
> *However it is amusing. I can hold my tongue with*
> *anyone, and the reporters who tackled me didn't get*
> *much for their pain. Among them was Weigall if you*
> *please – very fat and oily, and pretending to be a*
> *journalist only by accident so to speak.*

Arthur Weigall was an oddity among the reporters. When Carter lost his job as an Inspector of Antiquities, Weigall was the man who had stepped into his shoes. Since the Saqqara incident the two of them were not on friendly terms and Carter was a man who never forgot a grudge.

Weigall was out of a job and he turned up in Luxor as the *Daily Mail*'s special correspondent. As an expert, perhaps he hoped for special treatment. Instead, Carter treated him with frosty contempt. Weigall knew how to bear a grudge himself and soon became a poisonous enemy in the press camp. The foreign reporters in Luxor waged a constant war of rumour and lies against *The Times* agreement and Weigall entered into the battle with gusto. In his view, he'd come to Egypt to do a job and he was being prevented from getting on with it. Like the other reporters he objected to paying *The Times* for information and would use any means to get a story.

On 25 January, Weigall wrote to Carter offering him advice. He charged Carter and Carnarvon with acting more or less as they liked. Local gossip, he claimed, accused them of *"stealing some of the millions of pounds worth of gold of which you talked"* (a slur that would stick long afterwards). Weigall went on to attack *The Times* agreement and advised Carter to open his workshop to all reporters in order to *"tell the public what splendid work Lord Carnarvon is doing"*. Weigall's advice was hardly selfless, his real aim was to make his own job as a reporter easier. In any case Carter ignored every word. Even if Weigall was talking sense, Carter wouldn't have taken advice from him if he was the last man on Earth.

The fact remained that Carter was in an impossible position. He couldn't break the terms of *The Times* contract even if he wished. His only desire was to get on with the delicate work of recording and removing the objects from the antechamber. But Weigall and his cronies deliberately fanned the flames of discontent. They encouraged the outrage of the Egyptian newspapers while bombarding Carter's team with daily demands and complaints. They even appealed to Pierre Lacau, head of the Department of Antiquities, to help them break *The Times* monopoly.

Meanwhile the arguments raged back and forward

in the British press. On 10 February 1923, the *Daily Express* fumed:

> He [Lord Carnarvon] has not dug up the bones of his ancestors in the Welsh mountains. He has stumbled on a Pharaoh in the land of the Egyptians.... By making an exclusive secret of the contents of the inner tomb he has ranged against him the majority of the world's most influential newspapers...

The Times hit back six days later claiming the criticism of Carnarvon was unfair:

> He has been charged with creating a monopoly of news from Luxor, and even of commercialism ... no charge could be more false. He supplied the news through *The Times* solely because he thought it would be the best way, in fact the only practical way, of supplying it fully and independently to all newspapers throughout the world who wanted to take it.

The first casualty of the warfare was Carter. Day after day he made his procession through the crowds of tourists and reporters to the tomb entrance. Day after day he tried to ignore the constant complaints, requests and interruptions.

Lord Carnarvon, now back in the Valley, only added to Carter's frustrations. He was little help in the careful work of recording and preserving the objects. Instead he persisted in bringing his friends – titled earls and ladies – to see the tomb and generally get in the way. His lordship would talk and interfere in things he didn't understand. Arthur Mace's letters to his wife betray the first hint of the strain creeping into the relations between Carter and Carnarvon.

> *28th Jan 1923*
> *I fear from now on we shan't have so much quiet in our tomb work. It will take us all we know to restrain Carnarvon from plunging into things. Carter talks to him like a naughty child.*

> *7th Feb*
> *Carter's nerves are giving out with all the worry, and he'll have a breakdown if he isn't careful. Carnarvon makes all sorts of complications by doing things without thinking of the consequences. The Times contract has landed us in all sorts of trouble.*

Carter was under siege from all sides. Important people had to be shown around the tomb, including the Mayor of New York and the American Minister to Egypt. Throughout February the Egyptian government persisted in sending Carter a continual stream of visitors whom they expected him to make time for. Carter wrote:

> *There were days in which we actually had ten parties of visitors, and if we had given way to every demand there*

*would not have been a day in which we did not exceed the
ten. In other words there would have been weeks and
weeks at a time when no work would have been done at all.*

Each time another visitor arrived Carter had to smile,
pose for photos and play the tour guide, while inwardly
he fumed at another day's work lost. As his patience
wore thin, relations with Pierre Lacau and the
Department of Antiquities began to sour.

Official visitors weren't the only ones drawn to the
tomb. There were also the tourists. Carter's sudden
fame was a novelty at first, but he soon discovered that
celebrity came at a price. The small post office at Luxor
could hardly cope with the avalanche of letters and
telegrams that started to arrive. Throughout the winter
letters came tumbling in at a rate of up to a hundred a
week. Carter viewed this bombardment with a mixture
of bafflement and irritation: *"Beginning with letters of
congratulation, it went on to offers of assistance ...
fantastic money offers, from moving picture rights to
copyright on fashions..."*

Carter was pestered for *"a few grains of sand from
above the tomb"* and offered advice on everything from
preserving ancient statues to warding off evil spirits.
Some letter-writers even claimed to be related to him:
*"Surely you must be the cousin who lived in Camberwell in
1896 and whom we have never heard of since."* And so it
went on – and on. Everyone wanted to know Howard
Carter. He discovered a thousand "friends" who he

never had before. It was quite amazing for someone who had spent most of his 50 years living a quiet life by himself. Almost overnight Tutankhamun's tomb had become what Carter dreaded most – a tourist attraction. The Valley of the Kings had always attracted its share of tourists, but now it was one of the world's hot destinations. One English newspaper in January 1923 reported that more than 10,000 tourists were on their way to Egypt on big cruises. All of them planned to see Tutankhamun's tomb and most fondly imagined they could walk right into the tomb and see "*the Wonder of the World*" for themselves. Carter was horrified. All he wanted was to get on with the most important task of his life in peace.

In all the luxury hotels of Luxor the question on everyone's lips was "*Have you seen the tomb?*" Everyone claimed to know someone who knew Howard Carter and "*would be only too glad to provide a letter of introduction*". Carter soon developed a reputation for tearing the visiting cards of tourists into pieces. Even that didn't help. His prickly behaviour only added to his growing reputation.

Every morning Carter would make the short journey from his house to the tomb like a Hollywood movie star arriving for a film premiere. The crowds had come by horse-drawn carriage, on foot and by donkey. They seated themselves around the wall built around the tomb's entrance like picnickers in the park. Many of them relaxed under sunshades, swapping the latest stories from the paper, or eating breakfast from picnic baskets brought from their hotel. Carter made his way through this admiring crowd to cheers and applause. Every now and then he had to pause for handshakes or to have his photograph taken. He wore the air of a man who dearly wished he was invisible. The tourists tried every possible way to meet him and gain entry to the mysterious tomb. Some offered him large sums of money, others were more ingenious. One man tried to get into the tomb dressed as a telegraph boy, while another claimed to be selling lemonade. Travel companies eagerly cashed in on the Tutankhamun gold mine. In America package tours were sold, confidently *including* a viewing of the tomb. It was news to Carter – no one had asked him.

With enemies and interference on every side, Carter and his small team of experts closed ranks. Callender, Arthur Mace and Alan Gardiner have already been mentioned. The other three key figures in the story are Harry Burton, James Henry Breasted and Alfred Lucas.

Like Mace, Harry Burton, the team's photographer, was loaned from the Metropolitan Museum of New York. His photographs recorded the work stage by stage and provide a stunning record of Tutankhamun's tomb.

James Breasted, another American, was a respected Egyptologist from the University of Chicago. His son, Charles, made his own contribution to undermining *The*

Times monopoly by secretly sending reports to the *Chicago Daily News* from within the camp.

The final member of the team was Alfred Lucas, the Manchester-born chemist, who played a vital role in preserving the ancient objects found in the tomb.

This was the excavation team led by Howard Carter. Every day they worked in stifling heat that ranged from 24 – 29°C, facing some new problem in preserving thousands of fragile objects. It's no wonder there were outbursts of temper, angry words and periods of unprofessional sulking. Carter was usually at the centre of it, his temper as explosive as gunpowder.

Among those who suffered were two Americans, Walter Hauser and Lindsley Hall, who were loaned by the Metropolitan Museum of New York to make scale drawings in the antechamber. Both fell foul of Carter and eventually walked out.

Hall's diary for 20 January records *"a violent disagreement"* between him and Carter. At the time Carter was *"assisting"* Hall with his drawings, but the argument became so heated that Carter stormed off in a rage. A fortnight later Hauser also reached the end of his tether with Carter. *"Walter rowed with Carter and ended his work with him,"* says Hall's diary, sparing the details.

Despite this gloomy picture, Carter drove his team onwards towards a light at the end of the tunnel. After two months of hard work the antechamber was almost cleared. Each object or group of objects was numbered, labelled and photographed by Harry Burton where it was found. The thousands of objects and boxes were then removed to a storeroom in the nearby empty tomb of King Sety II. This wasn't as simple as it may sound. The guardian statues of the Pharaoh, for example, had to be tied to a large wooden stretcher, wrapped up and padded before they could be moved. In someone else's hands the whole job might have been done (badly) in a month, but Carter's thoroughness meant the entire clearance of the tomb would take years. At last – almost three months after the tomb was discovered – the antechamber was cleared. Carter could now turn his attention to the greatest prize of all – the king's burial chamber.

The date was set for the 16 February to take down the sealed door to the burial chamber. The public had followed every development in the newspaper's daily bulletins with mounting excitement. Everyone had been waiting for this moment with fevered anticipation. The excavators were anxious, the press fretted they might not be first with the news, the select few invited to the opening ceremony looked forward to the great day. One of Mace's letters to his wife reveals how the tension was affecting Carter personally.

I hope tomorrow will go off all right, for everybody's nerves are on edge, and Carter is on the verge of a nervous breakdown I should say. He and Carnarvon are on edge with each other all the time...

Carter did his best to control his impatience with official visitors and the Egyptian authorities. He found it harder to be patient with Carnarvon's interference and mistakes.

Since the start of the new year, tensions between the two men had been simmering below the surface. The fallout from *The Times* agreement was a daily reminder to Carter of his patron's mistake. To add insult to injury, he found himself denounced in the Egyptian newspapers for treating Tutankhamun's tomb as if it were his personal property. "*What right has an excavator to Egypt's sacred past?*" demanded the Cairo newspaper, *Al Ahram*. In the past Egypt's treasures had been carelessly ransacked by Europeans and Americans. Many rare pieces of ancient art had found a home in museums or private collections around the world. But the growing nationalist feeling in Egypt accused the "colonialists" of being little better than modern-day grave-robbers.

Carter bitterly resented such criticism. Not for a moment did he believe the tomb was "his" property. In his eyes it belonged to science and archaeology. He was simply doing his best to save it for future generations. If anyone was guilty of the charge it was Carnarvon. His patron was sticking to his claim to a share of the tomb's priceless treasures. In this Carter had flatly refused to support him. Having spent most of his life in Egypt, he had strong opinions of his own. The tomb of Tutankhamun was the greatest discovery of the age and couldn't be treated like any other tomb. According to

James Breasted, Carter felt passionately that such an important find should stay in Egypt where it belonged. With his usual bluntness no doubt he'd told Carnarvon he should give up any claim whatsoever.

The argument simmered on throughout February – with the tension threatening to erupt into something worse. In public Carter said nothing, but the cracks in the partnership were starting to show through.

For the time being, everything was set aside for the opening of the next chamber. Secretly, Carter knew for certain that Tutankhamun's shrine lay waiting for them beyond the sealed door. Two months before he had entered the chamber at night with Carnarvon and Lady Evelyn. On that occasion they had only glimpsed its shadowy outline by torchlight. What lay inside that vast mysterious shrine they now hoped to find out.

The Stage is Set

THE PAST TWO MONTHS had tried Carnarvon's patience. *The Times* deal had caused much more of an uproar than he could have imagined. Yet Lord Carnarvon still felt he'd acted for the best. Weren't the *Daily Mail* and the other papers showing their true colours in their disgraceful behaviour? Wouldn't it have been ten times more complicated to deal with every paper that demanded an interview? Relations with Carter were just as difficult. It was difficult not to get in the way of Carter's team while they worked on removing the fragile contents of the antechamber. As for Carter himself, he was like a volcano likely to erupt at any time.

As the day of the opening of the burial chamber drew nearer Carnarvon's nerves were on edge. No doubt he was worried that someone might inspect the robber's hole more closely and guess his guilty secret.

Nevertheless he'd been looking forward to this day for a long time. He had already glimpsed the burial chamber, but that had been in secrecy and darkness. Now Tutankhamun's shrine would be revealed before the whole waiting world and under the glare of lights. It was a great moment for Carnarvon – a day that would be talked about for many years to come.

Someone had to play the host on such an occasion and it was a role that suited Carnarvon. He was much more at home with an audience than Carter. The ceremony provided him with a welcome chance to step back into the spotlight as the patron and leader of the excavation. Maybe deep down, Carnarvon felt a sneaking sense of rivalry with his excavator, who had recently developed an irritating habit of talking to him as if he was an old fool.

Carter's refusal to support his claim to a share of the find was doubly annoying. His original concession to dig in the Valley stated he was entitled to a share of any less important pieces in a tomb, provided it had been robbed. It seemed plain enough to him that Tutankhamun's tomb fell into this category. But his whole case was undermined if Carter sided with the Egyptian government.

If Lord Carnarvon had decided to sell tickets to the opening of the burial chamber, he could have made a small fortune. In letters to the editor of *The Times* readers wanted to know what the famous discoverers expected to find behind the sealed wall. Wasn't it dangerous to enter the burial chamber of a Pharaoh?

Wouldn't they be cursed? More to the point, where could you buy tickets for the opening ceremony?

Only a select group were invited to the opening. Carnarvon had done his best to describe his expectations in an interview for *The Times*. His tone sounds remarkably cool, though his state of mind was anything but calm:

I shall expect [the shrine] to be of alabaster... I expect it will be filled with flowers and contain the royal regalia. In the sarcophagus I shall first expect to find the ordinary wooden coffin. Inside there will probably be a second coffin of thin wood, lined with finely chased silver. Inside this again, there will be a coffin of thin wood, richly gilt. There we shall find the mummy. It will be, I conjecture, encased in sheet gold about the thickness of the tin used for making tobacco boxes. The mummy will have gold bracelets at the wrists, gold rings at the ankles, a gold collar and breastplate, and a gold plate at the side where the abdomen was opened. His fingernails and toenails will be inlaid with gold. Enclosed with him in the coffins will probably be other precious royal objects. I shall also expect to find the richly ornamented vessels in which the heart and other internal organs are preserved, and it will, no doubt, have a finely worked portrait of the king on the lid.

How could Carnarvon know all this? Although he'd secretly entered the burial chamber, he certainly hadn't seen inside the shrine itself. In fact he was basing his predictions on an ancient Egyptian text, which gives a description of a Pharaoh's mummy. During the embalming process a cut was made in the side to remove the vital organs including the lungs and the liver. In the case of kings the cut was sealed with a gold plate. This much Carnarvon could predict. But the reality would turn out to be far more wonderful than he could imagine.

The press had worked themselves into a frenzy over the opening ceremony. They were not invited and Carnarvon had not even told them the exact day. Things had got so bad that he made no effort to keep the peace with the reporters. Rumours were going round that the sealed wall would be taken down in secret, without any officials present. Carnarvon could have cleared up this matter, but he chose not to, maybe enjoying a sense of mischief. For three or four days reporters haunted the entrance to the tomb, afraid to leave in case they missed the great event.

By now the opening ceremony was starting to resemble the first night of a grand opera, with Carnarvon playing the role of director. Behind a barrier in the antechamber chairs were set out in rows where the audience could watch the drama as it unfolded moment by moment. There was even a wooden stage where Carter would stand to attack the upper part of the plaster over the door. Lamps shone on the sealed doorway, bathing the whole stage in a theatrical glow.

Carnarvon must have given careful thought to the guest list. The antechamber was too small for a crowd, yet he had to be careful not to offend the Egyptian authorities by leaving anyone out. In the end he selected more than 20 people to invite to the opening including Pierre Lacau, Director of the Department of Antiquities and his inspectors. *The Times* reporter, Arthur Merton, smugly took his seat while his fellow reporters had to wait outside, feeding on scraps of information.

On the day, Carnarvon deliberately took the press and the tourists by surprise. The opening ceremony was fixed for the Friday afternoon. After lunch the invited guests met by secret appointment. The reporters guarding the tomb saw the procession arrive all of sudden out of nowhere. They guessed what it meant, but it was too late for them to make any special arrangements for sending messages to their editors.

Carnarvon took great pleasure in seeing the dismayed faces of the reporters as he arrived at the tomb. He was like a naughty schoolboy who had pulled off a clever a trick.

Arthur Weigall, the *Daily Mail*'s unpopular reporter, describes the scene dramatically:

> The wind suddenly got up as the party went down the steps, and it blew the hot white dust about, sending it up into the air in angry little scurries. One might almost have thought it to be connected in some way with the spirit of the dead Pharaoh,

petulant and alarmed at being disturbed, or perhaps annoyed at the jokes and laughter of some of the resurrection men, who had abandoned their silence and had become jocular as they went into the sepulchre [tomb]. A number of cane chairs had been taken down into the bare first room, so that the party could watch while the sealed wall was broken down; and Lord Carnarvon, perhaps overwrought by the excitement of the moment, made the jesting remark that they were going to give a concert down in the sepulchre. His words, though of little moment, distressed me, for I was absorbed, as it were, in my own thoughts, which were anything but jocular, and I turned to the man next to me and said: "If he goes down in that spirit, I give him six weeks to live".

Weigall's remark would prove to be more accurate than he could ever have imagined.

The First Blow

DOWN IN THE TOMB, Carter was ready to strip to his vest and trousers. If Lord Carnarvon was the director, he was the leading actor in this strange performance. He listened while Carnarvon made a brief speech thanking everyone for their work. Carter was less used to an audience and mumbled rather nervously through his own speech. He was anxious to get on with it. At last he was able to mount the stage to strike the first blow with a hammer and chisel.

Carter laboured with the help of Mace, chipping away at the sealed doorway bit by bit. It was an odd sensation standing on the stage and gradually widening the hole. As the heat in the tomb became more stifling, the tension in the air grew with every blow of Carter's hammer.

Above the tomb the reporters crowded around the entrance, straining to hear every sound echoing from the chamber. They watched each stone carried out of the tomb as if it was a vital clue to the mystery unfolding below.

Carter worked on in the stifling heat, trying to concentrate on the task. Occasionally he may have glanced in the direction of Carnarvon who was seated comfortably in the audience. Perhaps he reflected bitterly that it had been like this from the start. While Carnarvon kept at a comfortable distance in his Luxor hotel, Carter had to live with the daily trials of the Valley. There was plenty for him to brood upon. The war with the journalists was a constant thorn in his side, while relations with Pierre Lacau were increasingly strained. Normally Carter would have confided in his partner, but the two men were still at odds over the question of the tomb's treasures.

After about ten minutes of chipping away at the stones he had made a hole large enough to see through into the burial chamber. Just as on that first occasion, Carter pushed a torch into the hole and peered through. The sight was no less astonishing, even if he knew what to expect. On the other side, only about a metre from his face, was what seemed to be a wall of pure gold.

With renewed energy Carter went back to widening the hole with his hammer and chisel. The task wasn't as easy as it sounds. The stones in the plasterwork were rough slabs of different sizes, some so big that it took all Carter's strength to lift them. Once they were loose, one false move would have sent them crashing down into the next chamber, damaging what lay on the other side.

For the next two hours they settled into a system, Carter easing the stones in the plaster loose with a chisel and crowbar, while Mace held them to prevent them toppling into the burial chamber. When a stone was free they both lifted it out by hand and passed it back to Callender. The stone was then passed along a chain of workmen in the passageway and eventually out of the tomb.

Once a few more stones had been removed, the nature of the golden wall was clear. They were looking at one side of the majestic golden shrine of Tutankhamun. Caught in the beam of the lamps, the sight was so brilliant that Carter gazed in awe with everyone else. The audience had hoped for something wonderful, but none of them had expected this. Bit by bit, centimetre by centimetre, the golden shrine with its strange carvings was revealed.

After two hours of work, Carter and Mace were covered in dust and grime, their faces shining with sweat. Carter could see Carnarvon on the edge of his seat, eager for the moment when they could finally enter the next chamber. Yet, just when he thought the time had come, there was one more agonizing delay. On the threshold of the chamber they found a necklace probably dropped by the tomb robbers in their haste to escape. Beads had spilled everywhere and work had to be stopped whilst each one was gathered up by hand. It was a slow business and Carter felt his patience was close to snapping.

Finally it was done. The last stones were removed and the doorway to the chamber lay open.

Lord Carnarvon (left) and Howard Carter (right) at the Valley of the Kings excavation site.

The north wall of the antechamber with statues of the king guarding the entrance to a third chamber. The carefully placed basket conceals the robbers' hole that was secretly re-opened by Carter.

The antechamber of Tutankhamun's tomb, piled high with treasures.

*View of the treasury from inside the tomb showing the king's chest
in the background.*

Carter and Carnarvon open the wall of the burial chamber.

Tourists crowd around the site and watch as the treasures are removed from the tomb.

The Tutankhamun team photographed by Lord Carnarvon having lunch in a tomb. Seated from left to right: James Henry Breasted, Harry Burton, Alfred Lucas, Arthur Callender, Arthur Mace, Howard Carter and Alan Gardiner.

Howard Carter working on the third and innermost coffin of Tutankhamun. The burial oils, which had hardened into a pitch-like material, had to be carefully removed.

The innermost coffin of solid gold.

The unwrapped mummy of the boy-king, Tutankhamun.

In the Presence of the King

LORD CARNARVON FELT as if time had stood still. He had no idea how long they'd been sitting in that hot airless chamber, crowded with guests sweating in their jackets.

Now the moment had come he could hardly wait. So enormous was the shrine that it filled the burial chamber. In shape it was like a massive rectangular treasure chest with double folding doors at one end. It was made of wood covered with brilliant gold leaf. At nearly three metres tall, the shrine towered over him, almost touching the stone roof above. There was a gap of little more than half a metre between the walls of the chamber and the shrine where a person could edge past. It made it impossible for more than two or three people to enter the chamber at one time. Naturally Carnarvon proposed that he and Carter would go first, with Pierre Lacau, as the guest of honour, to accompany them.

They edged their way in, Carter uncoiling the wire of the lamp, so that they could take it into the dark chamber. The walls of the burial chamber were decorated with scenes painted in brilliant colours with inscriptions in *hieroglyphs* – the ancient writing of Egypt. But Carnarvon hardly noticed them. His whole attention was focussed on the immense shrine before him. The last time he had seen it, he'd had to make do with the narrow beam of a torch. Now in the glare of the electric light, he took his time to take in every startling detail.

There was no doubt it was one of the great royal shrines in which the kings of Egypt were laid. Made from thick panels of cedar, it was gilded with gold from top to bottom. Carved panels were inlaid with a brilliant blue and decorated with the signs of the gods Osiris and Isis. Along the sides of the shrine magic symbols were repeated to protect the shrine from evil spirits or enemies.

Surrounding the king's grave Carnarvon saw strange objects placed on the ground. Among these were a wooden goose, a lamp and an animal skin on a pole, filled with liquids for washing or preserving the body. In the narrow gap between the shrine and the chamber walls rested seven oars. The Egyptians believed that their dead king had to be ferried across to the next world in a boat. These were the magic oars Tutankhamun needed for his last great journey.

All of these things, Carnarvon would have taken in at a glance. But it was the magnificence of the shrine that took his breath away. He had seen it once before, but never in all its shining brilliance. He expected the shrine to be constructed like a series of Chinese boxes – four shrines, one inside the other. The last would be the sarcophagus itself containing the king's coffin.

Carnarvon had stood in this spot three months previously. Nevertheless he probably needed to reassure himself that Tutankhamun was there, inside. The outer shrine had no seal, which meant the tomb robbers could have broken into it.

Carnarvon held his breath as Carter drew back the ancient bolts made of ebony. Carved on the left-hand door was a strange headless, pawless creature with a lion's body. On the right sat a god in a feather head-dress. Carter swung back the heavy doors. Inside was a linen pall – a funeral cloth – brown with age. Beneath they found a second shrine with the doors bolted in the same way, but this time with a vital difference. The royal seal had not been broken. Carnarvon could breathe once again. The robbers had not opened the second shrine, Tutankhamun was still waiting for them.

It would have been tempting to go on, to fold back the doors until they reached the inner shrines and the coffin, but that would mean breaking the seal and they couldn't risk damage to the doors. Carter suggested they wait for another day and Carnarvon was forced to agree. In any case they had seen more than enough for one day. Instinctively Carnarvon found himself speaking in a hushed voice, feeling he was treading on holy ground.

With the opening of the doors it was impossible not to feel like an intruder. Inside this great golden monument lay the body of the dead king himself and they must show him respect.

Carefully they re-closed the great doors, and moved on to the far end of the chamber. Here one more surprise was in store for them. The tomb led into yet another chamber, smaller than the others beneath a low ceiling. The doorway hadn't been closed or sealed and at a glance it was clear that this room held Tutankhamun's most precious treasures.

Facing the doorway was the most breathtaking monument Carnarvon had ever encountered. Taller than a man, it was the king's chest, containing his liver and other organs removed from the body before mummification. The chest was guarded by the figures of four graceful goddesses, two of them looking back over their shoulders as if protesting at the intrusion. The monument dwarfed the other items in the room, which included golden chariots. Seated on a box like a watchdog, they saw a carved figure of the jackal-god, Anubis – guardian of the cemeteries. Elsewhere was a large number of beautiful chests, boxes and caskets. They opened one of these to reveal a beautiful ostrich feather fan. The feathers looked as if they had been plucked yesterday, waving gently in the draught from the open doorway of the chamber.

Did Carnarvon ever question his right to intrude on the dead Pharaoh that day? Not that we know. Certainly he must have felt the opening ceremony was a great personal triumph. He had promised his invited guests wonders – and Tutankhamun had not disappointed them.

As it turned out, the day would be Carnarvon's last great triumph, the pinnacle of his fame and success. The opening of the inner shrines and the king's coffin would be left to Howard Carter. Lord Carnarvon would never set eyes on the mummy of Tutankhamun.

Carter
Quarrel
16 February – 7 March 1923

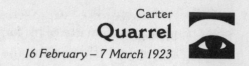

NONE OF THE GUESTS at the opening ceremony would have suspected the growing tension between Carter and his patron. In public they were the same as ever – Carnarvon quick to praise his partner's efforts, Carter consumed by the task before him. The cracks lay beneath the surface and could only be seen by those closest to Carter in his work team. Howard Carter could be short-tempered at the best of times, but his quarrel with Carnarvon went deeper than the odd outburst.

By the day of the opening ceremony Carter was a man on the verge of a nervous breakdown. He'd been working continually in the Valley for four months, having started early in November to escape the crowds of tourists. Normally Carter was used to a three-month season, but there had been no let-up from the huge demands of the work. He was exhausted. Something had to give way under the strain – and it was Carter's relationship with Carnarvon that snapped.

The row between the two reached a crisis soon after the opening ceremony. On 21 February, Carter received a visit from Carnarvon. He was used to his patron turning up at his house, but this time feelings were running high. Carter was in no mood for attempts to win him round. He was a broken man at the end of his tether. Rambling and mumbling, he paced the room complaining about the way he'd been treated. At some point Carnarvon may have brought up his claim to the treasures of the tomb. Whatever the cause, Carter lost his temper. Angry words were exchanged and all Carter's frustration of the last few months boiled over.

Two days later, a letter of apology came from Carnarvon. Carter made no reply. He didn't possess Carnarvon's generosity or his ability to forgive and forget. Carter's reputation for being tough and stubborn hid a sensitive man who easily took offence. Maybe all the years of biting his tongue and serving his master had taken their toll. Whatever the reasons he avoided company and brooded on his sense of betrayal.

Alan Gardiner and James Breasted both tried to plead Carnarvon's case with Carter but they only suffered his wrath as a result. *"A complete break seems inevitable,"* James Breasted commented gloomily. *"The man [Carter] is by no means wholly to blame. What he has gone through has broken him down."*

At the end of February, Carter must have been relieved when Carnarvon took a break and went off to Aswan. Carter stayed on in his house alone, nursing his bruised feelings and exhausted body. When Carnarvon returned from his trip in the first week of March, Carter received a second visit. But time had failed to heal any wounds. On this occasion it seems the argument went beyond harsh words. Carter, worked into one of his blazing furies, ordered his employer and patron out of his house. "Never come back!" was the sentiment of his final words.

Carnarvon never did return to his friend's house. As for Howard Carter, he probably regretted his harsh words for the rest of his life.

Death and the Curse

23 February – 5 April 1923

LORD CARNARVON WAS SHOCKED. He had always looked on Carter as his friend. For 14 years they'd worked together, finally achieving what every excavator dreamed of – the discovery of a royal tomb in all its glory. Now, in the very hour of triumph, their success had turned sour. For the moment Carnarvon had lost the one thing he'd always taken for granted – Carter's friendship.

Soon after his unhappy first visit to Carter's house (probably on Friday 23 February) Porchy sat down and wrote his old friend a letter of apology. He'd spoken with his daughter, Evelyn, who understood Carter better than he did, and was evidently feeling ashamed of himself.

> *I have been feeling very unhappy today and I did not know what to think or do, and then I saw Eve and she told me everything. I have no doubt that I have done many foolish*

*things and I am very sorry. I suppose the fuss and
worry have affected me but there is only one thing I
want to say to you which I hope you will always
remember – whatever your feelings are or will be for me
in the future my affection for you will never change. I'm
a man with few friends and whatever happens nothing
will ever alter my feelings for you.*

What exactly Porchy heard from his daughter remains
a mystery. Some have suggested that Evelyn had
revealed that she was secretly in love with Carter. The
forbidden romance adds a nice twist to the plot but
there's no real evidence for it. It's more likely that Evelyn
told her father that Carter was at the end of his tether
and Carnarvon was, in some ways, to blame. Carter was
certainly not himself. The man was visibly worn out by
the sheer hard labour of the last few months. Given time
and rest, Porchy felt his friend would cool down and they
could patch up their differences.

The letter was honest and heartfelt but no reply came
from Carter the next day or the one after. Porchy felt it
would be a good time for everyone to take a few days'
holiday from the work. That would give Carter some
breathing space. In any case the Valley was again plagued
with tourists and visitors from morning until night and
work was almost impossible.

Porchy and Evelyn were joined by Arthur Mace on the
short holiday. They sailed on the river, visited the tombs
and marvelled at the Aswan dam. Away from the

hothouse atmosphere of the Valley, Mace saw another side to his lordship: *"A queer fish, but in spite of his oddities very loveable,"* he wrote.

On his return to the Valley in the first week of March, Porchy made a second attempt to patch things up with Carter. He went to Carter's house with high hopes. But the meeting went disastrously wrong and he left with Carter's banishment ringing in his ears. It must have shocked him deeply to be barred from his friend's house. What had he done to deserve it? Carter seemed to be deaf to every attempt at making peace.

Time, in any case, was running out. On 6 March Carnarvon was bitten on the cheek by a mosquito. He paid little attention to it at the time. But later, while shaving in his room at the Winter Palace Hotel in Luxor, he accidentally opened the wound with his cut-throat razor. He treated the wound, but it became infected and he was soon running a raging temperature of 38.3°C. Evelyn insisted that he take to his bed to rest and recover.

Two days later, on 8 March, Carnarvon was evidently feeling well enough to return to getting in the way of the work at the tomb. But events were swiftly heading towards their tragic conclusion.

On 14 March Carnarvon went to Cairo. There he met up with his old friend, Alan Gardiner. By this time the warning signals were clear. The two dined at a club. Porchy was looking tired and ill but insisted on going on to see a film. It was the last time he was ever out of doors.

Ever since his near-fatal car accident, Carnarvon had suffered from regular bouts of illness. Now the infected mosquito bite led to blood poisoning, which worsened to become pneumonia. Evelyn's letter to Carter of 18 March betrays her anxiety for her father:

> *I've made a point of making light of it to most people as I don't want an exaggerated account in the papers. Of course they may never get hold of it at all but since you've all become celebrities I feel there is nothing one does or thinks that they don't know! But I like you knowing exactly what's happening to us. We miss you and I wish Dear you were here.*

The papers soon got wind of the news. Nothing could be whispered in Luxor without it being broadcast around the world the very next day. The newspapers ran daily bulletins on Carnarvon's state of health, which was rapidly getting worse. By 19 March Evelyn sent a telegram to Carter, saying that she was seriously alarmed and had wired for her mother to come. Days later Lady Carnarvon arrived in a Puss Moth aeroplane, bringing the family doctor, Johnson. Carter himself broke off work and went to Cairo to see if he could be of any help. There were times when Carnarvon rallied, and a stronger man might have pulled through. But Carnarvon's body was worn out by recent events and years of illness.

A letter from Alan Gardiner to his wife, on 1 April, suggests the shadows were gathering:

I have just come back from seeing Evelyn; it has been a bad day and he had a terrible crisis just before six o' clock this evening, I was quite miserable about it ... why am I so fond of him? And that poor little girl nearly breaks my heart with her devotion. There she sits, day and night, tired out and waits ready to run to him... The crisis must come in a short time now... He wanted to see me last night, but of course they wouldn't let me. I do so want him to pull through.

Four days later – on 5 April 1923 – Lord Carnarvon died. He was 57 years old.

The newspapers were quick to cast a sinister light on his death. Carnarvon, they reported, was a victim of the mummy's curse.

Rumours began to appear in print. On the very day the tomb was opened, the papers reported, Carter's pet canary was swallowed by a cobra. (It was well known that the cobra was the royal snake, which crowned a Pharaoh's head-dress, ready to spit fire at his enemies.) Other reports claimed that, at the moment of Carnarvon's death, the lights of Cairo had gone out without warning. While, over in England, his lordship's three-legged terrier, Susie, howled and dropped dead on the spot. All these stories had witnesses who were prepared to vouch for their truth.

The rumours all added fuel to the legend of the curse. Carnarvon had been present when the Pharaoh's burial chamber had been disturbed – he had even laughed and joked on the occasion. Those with vivid imaginations even claimed that Carnarvon had pricked his finger on an object left in the tomb by its ancient guardians. To many, it was clear that the mummy's curse had claimed its first victim.

The curse would grow into a legend discussed for years to come. It sold newspapers and for once, *The Times* had no monopoly on the story. Yet was there any real mystery surrounding Carnarvon's death?

The facts show that Porchy was not a strong man. He had gone to Egypt for the sake of his health, which was always delicate at best. That, of course, didn't stop people believing in the curse. Newspapers quoted an imaginary inscription from the tomb: *"Death shall come on swift wings to him that toucheth the tomb of Pharaoh."* Two weeks before Carnarvon died, the novelist Marie Corelli had warned that *"the most dire punishment follows any rash intruder into a sealed tomb."* Her fellow writer, Arthur Conan Doyle, also saw dark forces at work. He claimed Carnarvon's death was caused by dark spirits, created by Tutankhamun's priests to guard the tomb.

The widespread belief that the tombs of Pharaohs are protected by curses is based on some real evidence. In the tomb of Harkhuf – which Carnarvon may have seen in Aswan – a warning on the wall reads: *"Whoever enters this tomb ... on him will I pounce as on a bird, he shall be judged for it by the great god."* The dire warnings were put there to frighten off any would-be tomb robbers. The ancient Egyptians viewed tomb theft as a monstrous crime. The tomb and mummy were the earthly dwelling of the *Ka* – the life-force of the person – which lived on after death. Plundering a tomb made the *Ka* homeless and nameless.

Some of the strange stories are hard to explain. During Carnarvon's fever, it's said that he repeated, *"A bird is scratching my face. A bird is scratching my face."* One expert pointed out that a curse text warns that the vulture goddess, Nekhebet, shall scratch the face of anyone who does anything to a tomb.

The story of the lights going out all over Cairo at the time of Carnarvon's death was certainly true. Carnarvon's young son, who would become the 6th Earl, was there at his father's bedside and remembers the hotel being plunged into darkness. It was probably just an odd coincidence and power cuts were not uncommon. Believers in the curse pointed to another factor – the startling number of deaths connected with the tomb.

The list of the supposed victims of the curse is a long one and it would occupy too much space to detail them all. Among the better known victims are Carnarvon's younger brother, Aubrey, who died unexpectedly later that year, and Arthur Mace, Carter's trusted assistant, who suffered a breakdown of health and died before work in the tomb was finished. A British radiologist – Archibald Reed – died on the way to Luxor in 1924 to X-ray a mummy, though not Tutankhamun. The American railroad owner Jay Gould died of pneumonia, said to be the result of a cold he caught while visiting the tomb. Yet another who saw Tutankhamun's grave and came to a nasty end was the Egyptian Ali Kemel Fahmy Bey. He was later shot by his wife in London's Savoy hotel. Each of these mysterious incidents fed the public's appetite for the legend of the curse. How could such a catalogue of death be mere coincidence?

Ten years later, Egyptologist Herbert Winlock, decided to test the curse theory for his own amusement. He found that of the 26 people who had actually witnessed the opening of the king's burial chamber, only *two* had in fact died. Many of them, including Harry Burton, Lady Evelyn and Alan Gardiner lived on to a ripe old age. If the Pharaoh's curse existed, it was strangely selective in its choice of victims. After Carnarvon, the next man to be struck down should logically have been Howard Carter – yet he would live on to the age of 64. The last word goes to Carter himself, who typically scorned any talk of a curse. *"All sane people should dismiss such inventions with contempt,"* he bristled.

Carter Alone

5 April 1923 – 18 February 1924

"POOR LORD C DIED during the early hours of the morning," Carter wrote in his diary. What he really felt he never said. He stayed in Luxor right to the end – until his old friend's body left Cairo to be taken for burial in England. In his will Carnarvon had asked to be buried on Beacon Hill overlooking Highclere Castle, *"if possible and if it does not cost more than fifty pounds"*. To the very end his lordship kept strict accounts of expenses.

When Carter finally returned to work on 16 April, he looked tired and worn out. Perhaps what he felt most was abandonment. His partnership with Carnarvon had survived 14 years, through good fortune and bad. It had started out as master and employee, but in time grew into a deep friendship between two very different and unusual men. If Carnarvon had few real friends, Carter had even fewer.

Carter probably wished he'd never spoken those angry words on that unhappy day at his house. He must have gone back over that exchange many times in his head. Away from the hothouse of the Valley the pair might have had time to heal the wounds. But death's timing is cruel – barely a month after their argument, Carnarvon was gone.

Carter had lost his partner, patron and, perhaps, his most loyal friend. He found himself alone and finally in command. Up to now, Carnarvon had stood as a buffer between Carter and the authorities. Porchy had been one of a dying generation – an aristocrat of the old school. Sometimes he showed the arrogance of his class, for instance in his scornful attitude to Egyptians. At times he made bad decisions, rushing in when he should have listened to advice. Yet, with all his faults, he was good company, charming, generous and – as Mace said – "loveable". These were qualities that Howard Carter lacked. The situation he faced was about to become dogged by politics. Many difficult questions surrounding the tomb still had to be answered. Carnarvon couldn't have died at a worse time.

Following Carnarvon's sudden death, Carter spent the summer in England. It was easy enough to persuade Lady Almina Carnarvon to renew the concession to the tomb under her own name. She was willing to continue funding the work but would be little more than a figurehead. In Egypt, Carter would be firmly in charge, with no one to restrain his stubborn nature.

By the autumn of 1923 he was looking forward to throwing himself back into his work with new energy. The next stage of the work would involve opening the four golden shrines to reveal the coffin containing the actual mummy. Since the shrines sat tightly, one within the next, it posed a tricky problem. There was still so much to do before the clearance of the tomb was complete. While the antechamber had been cleared there still remained everything in the treasury and the smaller annexe room. Every object had to be numbered, recorded, photographed and carefully wrapped for transport. Yet if Carter imagined he could get on with his work in peace he was sadly mistaken. His problems had only just begun.

Since the war Egypt had been a British Protectorate, which meant that in effect Britain ruled Egypt and told the government what to do. However, a nationalist movement had been gaining ground, demanding independence and an end to British rule. By 1924, with a general election due, the Nationalists were the strongest party. The end of the British Protectorate released a great flood of national pride. The tomb of Tutankhamun became a cause to beat the patriotic drum and Carter would be a victim of the changing times.

Carter paid little attention to politics, he had more pressing problems. The first concerned *The Times* agreement. Surprisingly Carter advised Lady Almina to renew the exclusive contract and went even further. He adopted *The Times* reporter, Arthur Merton, as a full member of his team. Merton would give daily bulletins to *The Times* in the evening, and then to the Egyptian press the next morning, so that the news would reach the public in London and Cairo practically at the same time.

Since *The Times* deal had brought him nothing but trouble, Carter's decision is hard to fathom. It's likely that he felt bound by his dead friend's wishes. Promises had been made by Carnarvon and would be honoured. In any case, Carter was in no mood to hand out favours to the foreign journalists who'd behaved so badly the previous season. Renewing *The Times* deal was Carter's first bad mistake – adding to the growing ranks of his enemies.

Carter's second problem concerned visitors to the tomb. In talks with Pierre Lacau, head of the Department of Antiquities, he offered to open the tomb to the public for a week whenever a convenient halt in the work arose. Otherwise tourists would have to apply to the Department for entry permits. It was a vague arrangement, but Carter hoped it would protect him from constant interruption. He was sadly wrong. Lacau – under pressure from the mischief-making journalists – kept changing and adding to the terms of the agreement. "*Shilly-shallying,*" Carter called it, in disgust.

By 17 November 1923 Carter and Mace were back at work. To their annoyance a steady flow of visitors turned up at the tomb with permits from the Department. Once again Carter felt he was being treated as a glorified tour guide. A letter from Arthur Mace on 26 November describes the worsening relations with Pierre Lacau and the Department:

> *All the trouble started up afresh, and impossible restrictions were being put upon Carter. The matter was fought out for a fortnight and finally a compromise was agreed on, which may or may not work. Carter was within an ace of closing up the tomb and refusing to go on with it. Lacau was all up in the air, agreed to a thing one day and contradicted it the next... The whole Department seems to have gone clear off their heads.*

Carter's impatience was understandable. He needed peace and quiet, but instead he got constant interruption.

The Department struck the next blow in the war of words. They demanded a full list of Carter's staff, claiming the right to bar anyone they didn't approve of from the tomb. The obvious target was Merton – *The Times* reporter whose privileged position was bitterly resented by the rest of the press pack. Carter dug in his heels, at first refusing to submit a list. Lacau's reply that *"the Government no longer discusses but conveys to you its decision"* – marked a raising of the stakes. In other words Carter was being told to obey orders. If Lacau was trying to force Carter out of the tomb altogether, he was going the right way about it. A fight was in the air and in Carter's mind the whole future of archaeology in Egypt was at stake.

For now, a truce was called for an important event. Carter was ready to draw back the doors of the remaining shrines to discover what lay inside. He had already seen inside the outer two shrines, the third and fourth remained. (In all Tutankhamun was protected by eight layers – four shrines, the sarcophagus and, inside that, three coffins.) The opening of the two inner shrines took place in the new year, on 3 January 1924. The funeral pall – made of thin fabric – posed the most difficult problem since it was likely to fall apart the moment it was touched. Carter, with help from Dr Alexander Scott of the British Museum, found a way of strengthening the fabric so it could be wound on a wooden roller and removed. Once this was done the bolts of the third and fourth inner shrines could be drawn back. Carter held his breath.

The decisive moment was at hand! An indescribable moment for the archaeologist! What was beneath and what did that fourth shrine contain? With intense excitement I drew back the bolts of the last and unsealed doors, they slowly swung open, and there, filling the entire area within, effectually barring any further progress, stood an immense yellow quartzite sarcophagus, intact, with the lid still firmly fixed in its place, just as the pious hands left it.

The sarcophagus was carved from a single block of sandstone, the *"yellow quartzite"* described by Carter. At each corner stood figures of the four protective goddesses – Isis, Nephthys, Neith and Selkis – their wings outstretched, enfolding the sarcophagus in a shield of protection. It was a breathtaking sight and confirmed to Carter once and for all that Tutankhamun lay within, unharmed. But before the lid of the sarcophagus could be raised, the four golden shrines would have to be dismantled.

Over the next weeks the delicate work progressed. Work in the burial chamber demanded endless patience. Carter records, *"We bumped our heads, nipped our fingers, we had to squeeze in and out like weasels, and work in all kinds of embarrassing positions."*

The task was made harder by orders from Lacau and constant visits. Carter still found his way to the tomb blocked every morning by crowds of tourists. He even resorted to stealing into the tomb before sunrise to avoid them. Once his trick was discovered the tourists would wait outside and chant his name – "Carter, Carter!" until he appeared at the entrance and granted them a weary wave of the hand. He never really understood what all the fuss was about, believing the tomb was chiefly of interest to archaeologists.

At last the day drew near for the opening of the sarcophagus. It was the day that Carter had worked towards for over a year. The day when the full glory of Tutankhamun's tomb would be revealed. But Carter would not enjoy his triumph for long. The feud with the Department of Antiquities was about to erupt into open warfare.

The date for the lifting of the lid was set for 14 February 1924. James Breasted was present, along with Mace, Callender, Alan Gardiner and Harry Burton who would record the historic moment on cine-film. The Egyptian government and the Department would also be well represented.

When the time came the air was heavy with memories. No one could ignore the echoes of that happier day a year ago when Carnarvon was present to open the burial chamber. At lunch Carter sat at the head of the table, in the seat Carnarvon used to take. He looked exhausted and admitted that he felt ill.

Carter had installed a pulley system to raise the heavy lid of the sarcophagus. It was a risky procedure since the stone slab weighed one-and-a-half tonnes and a large crack ran through the middle. One false move and the heavy lid would come crashing down – destroying the coffin and the king's remains for ever.

Just after three o' clock the sombre group gathered in the tomb. The elaborate pulley system was in place. The ropes tightened and began to take the strain of the one-and-a-half tonne granite lid. Harry Burton cranked the handle on his camera. What would they find inside?

Slowly, and swaying a little, the stone lid began to rise.

At first Carter could see nothing but empty darkness. Then he gradually made out fragments of granite, which had fallen out of the crack in the lid. They were scattered upon a dark shroud, which covered a form that wasn't yet clear.

The ropes were stretching. When the hoists had been drawn up as far as the low ceiling allowed, the heavy lid was swinging not more than half a metre above the sarcophagus. Carter turned his flashlight on what lay within. He announced that the coffin inside was resting upon a stand in the form of a golden lion. There followed a complete silence. James Breasted was reminded of the sudden stillness at a funeral:

> *Carter and Mace stepped quietly forward to the head of the sleeping figure and loosening the shroud on either side, slowly and carefully rolled it back off the head towards the feet... We suddenly saw the gleaming gold of the vulture's head and the upreared cobra on the King's forehead. We saw his eyes, which seemed to look out upon us as in life, and soon the King's whole figure was revealed to us in all the splendour of shining gold.*

Of all the marvels the tomb had shown them, this was the most breathtakingly beautiful. The coffin was a portrait of the king lying stretched out, "*like a crusader on his tomb slab in some European cathedral,*" according to Breasted. The golden coffin was 2.24 metres long, taller than a man, and glittered with sheet gold from head to foot. It pictured the Pharaoh as the god Osiris, king of the dead, with the divine cobra curled on his head-dress. His arms were crossed, holding the symbols of kingship – the crook and the flail.

The whole operation of raising the lid had taken less than an hour and was a triumph for Carter. Afterwards, with the tension of the past weeks forgotten, Carter took the whole party for a celebration in the empty tomb of Ramesses XI – where he raised a toast to their success.

Carter had no time to enjoy his triumph. Before breakfast the next morning he received news that left him thunderstruck. That day he had invited the wives of his English and American team to view the tomb, but before they could go a note arrived from Mohammed Zaghul, Under-secretary in the Ministry of Works. It said that the wives were forbidden to enter the tomb. The government ruled that they needed to apply for a permit from the Ministry like everyone else. Pierre Lacau had signed the documents, feebly protesting that he had no choice but to follow government orders. As early as dawn, police were on duty outside the tomb to prevent anyone entering without permission.

It was a slap in the face and Carter took it for a deliberate insult. For over a year he had laboured with his team in the tomb *he* had discovered. Now the government presumed to tell him who could and couldn't enter. It was too much. Coming on top of the accusations, arguments and the endless interruptions, this was the last straw. Carter had reached the end of his patience.

Shortly after eight, he arrived at Mace's house looking pale and ill. A counsel of war was held at the Winter Palace Hotel, where Carter and Mace were joined by their colleagues, including James Breasted and Alan Gardiner. Having failed in their request for a meeting with the Minister, they attempted to draw up a written statement. Charles Breasted wrote while Carter paced up and down, firing off angry sentences. The statement had to go through 20 different versions as the others tried to tone down Carter's wild threats and abuse.

In the end they agreed on a dignified declaration of war:

> Owing to the impossible restrictions on the part of the Public Works Department and its Antiquities Service, all my collaborators in protest have refused to work any further upon the scientific investigations of the discovery of the tomb of Tutankhamun.
>
> I therefore am obliged to make known to the public that, immediately after the Press view of the tomb this morning, between 10 am and noon, the tomb will be closed, and no further work can be carried out.
>
> Howard Carter

The tomb would be closed. Carter was all for filling it in entirely, but he was persuaded to stop short of such drastic action. He was at the end of his tether. Exhausted and unwell, he felt the ban on the wives' visit was an insult not only to him, but also to his team and to Lady Carnarvon. By itself the incident might have been smoothed over, but for weeks Carter had been pushed beyond the limits of his patience. Sooner or later he was bound to snap. It was the first strike in the history of archaeology.

Carter's announcement was displayed in the lobby of the Winter Palace Hotel in Luxor. At last the tourists and the reporters had a real scandal to talk about.

It must be asked whether the Egyptian government deliberately pushed Carter over the edge. They might have guessed how he would react to the order and the fact was the strike played into their hands. By walking out, Carter broke the terms of Lady Carnarvon's concession, and Lacau could argue it was cancelled. In the long run, closing the tomb was Howard Carter's worst mistake. The conflict quickly became a legal battle and in law the Egyptian government held all the aces. Carter found himself outside of the tomb and powerless to get back in.

Much later, Carter was able to admit he might have made a mistake:

No man is wise at all times – perhaps least of all the archaeologist who finds his efforts to carry out an all absorbing task frustrated by a thousand pinpricks and irritations without end.

Meanwhile, in all the trading of insults, one vital matter had been forgotten: the stone lid still hung by ropes over Tutankhamun's sarcophagus. In his rage Carter had closed the tomb without lowering it –

perhaps thinking the dispute wouldn't last long. If the ropes frayed and broke, one-and-a-half tonnes of stone would come crashing down on the coffins containing the mortal remains of Tutankhamun. Everything would be lost. Carter asked for permission to enter the tomb to make the lid safe, but Lacau refused. So the lid remained suspended in the air, and with it, Carter's nerves hung by a thread.

The Mummy Revealed

15 February 1924 – 11th November 1925

HOWARD CARTER WAS IN DESPAIR. How had it come to this? In November 1922 his name had echoed round the world as the hero of the greatest find of the century. The tomb had become his life's work – the task that drove him on, threatening his health and peace of mind. He had battled on in the stifling heat of the Valley, despite the daunting scale of the task and the loss of his friend and partner, Lord Carnarvon. Now it looked as if it was all over. He was a forlorn figure, worn out and bewildered by the way he'd been treated. The future looked gloomy and uncertain.

Meanwhile, in the tomb, the heavy sarcophagus lid still hung by ropes where Carter had left it. For a whole week the possibility of disaster preyed on Carter's nerves as the situation was allowed to drag on. Pierre Lacau blamed Carter for leaving the lid unsecured, but did nothing to make it safe.

On 22 February, Lacau finally cut through the padlocks and broke into the tomb. To everyone's relief, he found that the ropes had stretched so far that the lid had lowered itself almost back into place on top of the sarcophagus. No thanks to modern man, Tutankhamun was safe.

From this point the Egyptian government officially took over the tomb and reopened it to visitors. They marked the occasion with a fireworks display. Meanwhile two of Carter's faithful Egyptian foremen lingered near the entrance to the tomb, guarding a pile of their master's property.

What was Carter to do now? The lawsuit with the Egyptian government dragged on, attempting to rescue Lady Carnarvon's rights over the tomb. But there was little hope of winning. On 9 March 1924, Carter signed a document promising that he would never lay any claim to any of the objects found in the tomb. Soon after, he left Egypt for England, with the prospect of a lecture tour in America ahead of him. For the time being, he was quitting the field.

Howard Carter might never have returned to Tutankhamun's tomb if a shocking event hadn't re-opened the door. On 19 November 1924, Sir Lee Stack – the Commander-in-Chief of the British army – was shot dead by a terrorist on the doorstep of his home in Cairo. The Nationalist government got the blame and the outraged British took control of Egypt once again. The Nationalists were forced out of power and, in one stroke, Carter's main enemy was removed from the scene.

The new government, led by Prime Minister Ziwar Pasha, wanted to build bridges. Carter returned to Egypt and fortune smiled on him once again. He happened to run into the Prime Minister at the Continental Hotel where he was staying. Ziwar Pasha immediately raised the subject of the tomb and they both agreed it was important to settle the problems for the good of tourism as well as archaeology.

Within weeks Carter sent a telegram to Lady Carnarvon. A deal had been struck over the division of the tomb's treasures. In fact Carter had agreed to climb down from Carnarvon's original demands. Lady Almina would give up her claims to the treasures of the tomb in return for a few minor objects where two or more identical copies existed. *The Times* agreement was another casualty of Carter's weaker bargaining position.

The way was now clear for Howard Carter to return to the Valley. Even Lacau breathed a sigh of relief. The truth was no one else wanted to take on the mammoth task of clearing the tomb. While the Egyptian government had locked Carter out, they didn't possess anyone to replace him. From the very start Tutankhamun was Carter's obsession and no one else could reliably complete his work.

When Carter returned on 22 January 1925, he found his work in a state of neglect. The tomb was covered in a layer of rubbish about half a metre deep and there was worse to come. The beautiful linen pall that had covered the king's grave had been left outside in the sun and wind.

All that remained of the 3,000-year-old burial shroud were a few shreds of decaying fabric. It was Egypt's loss not his, Carter told himself.

The rest of the burial chamber remained as Carter had left it, with the coffins still unopened within the sarcophagus. Since Carter and his team had gone on strike in February 1924, almost a year had been wasted. Tutankhamun remained in his coffin, still undisturbed. The final act was still to be played. In what state would they find the mummy?

Carter was now entering uncharted territory. In fact he was dealing with a nest of three wooden coffins, one sitting inside the other, like Russian dolls. Each coffin was delicately carved and painted with gold, shining like the scales of a fish. Inside the third and final coffin he expected to find the mummy of Tutankhamun himself.

The opening of the coffins would test Carter's skill to the limit. They nested so tightly inside each other that it was impossible to even pass a finger between them. To complicate matters, the Egyptian priests had poured oils over the coffin at the time of the burial. These offerings to the gods had set hard as cement. Just as before, the answer lay in a pulley system to lift the coffins free centimetre by centimetre. Even then Carter found it a nerve-racking process.

Everything may seem to be going well when suddenly you hear a crack. Little pieces of surface ornament fall. Your nerves are at an almost painful tension. What is happening? All available room in the narrow space is crowded with your men. What is needed to avert a catastrophe?

Thanks to Carter's skill, the three coffins were eventually removed without harm. It was slow, painstaking work, which lasted until November 1925. Each coffin was in human form with the lid carved to represent the boy Pharaoh, his arms crossed and holding the crook and the flail. The king's portrait wore the false beard and the royal head-dress, entwined with the cobra and the vulture.

When the third and last coffin was revealed it was folded in a shroud of red linen. The face was left bare with a delicate collar of blue glass beads, flowers, berries and fruit. But this wasn't the only surprise awaiting Carter.

An astounding fact was disclosed. The third coffin ... was made of solid gold! The mystery of the enormous weight, which hitherto had puzzled us, was now clear... Its weight was still as much as eight strong men could lift.

In fact the solid gold coffin tipped the scales at 110.4 kilograms. Its scrap value alone today would be worth well over £1 million. All the same, the gold at first looked black. Carter estimated that two buckets of thick anointing oil had been poured over the coffin. It had set solid and stuck to the base of the second coffin. This had to be painstakingly removed by hammering and using fierce heat – a risky business at any time.

At last, Carter was ready to lay bare the tomb's final secret – the mummy itself. In his account Carter declared, *"we were in the presence of the dead king and must do him reverence."* Perhaps he felt torn between respect for the king and curiosity to know what lay inside the final coffin. The ancient Egyptians had gone to great lengths to protect the body of their king from any intruder. Tutankhamun's remains lay within eight boxes, including the stone sarcophagus. Now Carter was about to draw back the final curtain to gaze at something no eye had seen for 3,000 years. How would he find the boy-king?

Carter never stopped to ask if he had any right to disturb the body of an ancient king. He talked of respect but the demands of science and curiosity were stronger than any doubts. *"The emotional side is no part of archaeological research,"* he declared.

Ten gold pins had to be removed before the upper half of the third coffin could be lifted free. Spellbound, Carter gazed at last on the mummy revealed inside. There was the small body, tightly bandaged and covered with thick anointing oils, blackened by age. But what magnetized their attention was something amazing. The head was covered by a stunning gold death mask – a portrait of the king staring back at them. The striped head-dress was gold and vivid blue and the large, painted eyes were disturbingly life-like. As a work of art, it was more beautiful than anything Carter had ever seen.

Still Tutankhamun's face resisted them. When Carter tried to remove the mummy and mask from the coffin he found that both were stuck fast to the bottom of the coffin. To prise them free would risk damaging both the mummy and the death mask.

It was decided that the mummy would have to be examined in the coffin where it lay.

The coffin was carried into the empty tomb of Sethos, where, on 11 November 1925, a small party gathered to witness the examination of Tutankhamun's remains. Many of Carter's original team were missing from this final act of the drama. Lord Carnarvon was dead and Carter's right-hand man, Arthur Mace, had fallen seriously ill. There was no Alan Gardiner or James Breasted present. Only Harry Burton remained, taking the photographs that provide a wonderfully detailed record of the tomb.

Alfred Lucas, the English chemist, helped Carter unwind the bandages slowly and carefully. They were fragile and would fall to pieces at the slightest touch, so had to be strengthened by painting them with wax.

The spectators moved in closer as Dr Douglas Derry, a surgeon, made the first cut with a scalpel. Then the outer layers were peeled back like the skin of an orange. As each layer of bandages was unwound, pieces of jewellery and amulets (charms) fell out of the folds. They were bound on to the king's body to ward off evil powers. From the 13 layers between the throat and stomach alone, Howard Carter removed 35 amulets. Around the body Carter found gold plaques bearing speeches from the gods and goddesses. These greetings to the young Pharaoh were magic spells to ensure he would live for ever. As the son of Re, the sun god, the Egyptians believed their young king would journey to the underworld to join the other gods and goddesses.

At last the final bandages were unwound and the mummy itself lay before them. This was the moment Carter had been anticipating for three years. In fact the body he found was pathetically small, the skin leathery and greyish. The head was cleanly shaven, suggesting Tutankhamun had recently been visited by the royal barber. The ears were pierced while the nose had been flattened by the pressure of the bandages. The eye sockets were empty, though that didn't stop Carter imagining the king was looking at him. The arms looked as if they were folded and the teeth were bared in a hideous smile.

The examination found that Tutankhamun was a boy of no more than 16 or 17 when he died. The body was 1.63 metres tall (5 feet 4 inches) – exactly the height of the two guardian statues at the entrance to the burial chamber. As Carter wrote:

> The youthful Pharaoh was before us at last... Here was the climax of our long researches! The tomb had yielded its secret: the message of the past had reached the present in spite of the weight of time, and the erosion of so many years.

And what was the message of the past, that Carter thought he heard? Perhaps, that for all the efforts of science, the boy inside the tomb remained as mysterious as the Sphinx itself. Dr Derry was unable to suggest a cause of the king's early death. A series of X-rays taken later, in 1968, revealed a small fragment of bone within the Pharaoh's skull. It seemed that the king might have died from a blow to the head. But whether it was murder or the result of an accident, the scientists couldn't say.

That was one secret Tutankhamun refused to give up.

Afterword

THE DISCOVERY OF Tutankhamun's tomb changed the lives of Howard Carter and Lord Carnarvon for ever. From the moment the find was reported in *The Times* the two men were guaranteed a place in history. But while the tomb brought them fame, it certainly didn't bring good fortune.

Tutankhamun *made* Howard Carter, and afterwards would never let him go. Before November 1922 his name would have hardly been known outside of a small corner of Egypt. Afterwards he was treated like a film star and sat down to lunch with royalty. Tutankhamun lifted the poor excavator from Norfolk into a social world that had previously totally ignored him.

Carter felt Tutankhamun was his responsibility and for seven more years he worked on, preserving and recording the objects he'd discovered. He wasn't able to leave the tomb for good until 1935. His three-volume book, *The Tomb of Tutankhamun*, appeared in 1933. But it was only a popular version of the story written up from Carter's notes by his close friend Percy White. For the rest of his days Carter worked on a proposed six-part scholarly account – "A Report upon the Tomb of Tutankhamun" – which would stand as a monument to his life's work.

Unlike Carter, Lord Carnarvon needed no introductions to royalty. As an English aristocrat he already moved in the highest circles. Fame didn't interest him, but the tomb promised something better still. Just as he sought out the fastest cars and racehorses, he wanted his Egyptian collection to contain the best artefacts. The tomb offered untold treasures and he always believed that a share rightfully belonged to him.

In the end Carnarvon's hopes were bitterly disappointed. Despite vague promises, he never received one single object from Tutankhamun's tomb. (Most of the treasure was moved to Cairo Museum, while the mummy remained in his tomb.) In 1930 his widow, Lady Carnarvon, received a cheque for £36,000 from the Egyptian government to cover her expenses on the excavation. With that, the authorities considered the matter closed. Porchy, if he'd survived, might have managed a hollow laugh at how it all turned out.

He never lived to see the mummy of the Pharaoh whose shrine he had touched. In the end, Tutankhamun had cost him not only his friendship with Carter but his life. The partnership never had time to recover from its lowest point before Carnarvon became ill and died.

Howard Carter lived on but, after he returned to England in 1932, he seemed worn out. Years of working in the desert, often underground, together with the trials of his discovery had ruined his health. His great six-volume book was never completed or published. In later years he was largely forgotten and neglected by the public. In America and Europe he received honorary degrees for his achievement but in his own country he was ignored. He never received a knighthood – perhaps because he made too many enemies during his career. To the end Carter remained an awkward outsider. He died at his Kensington home on 2 March, at the age of 64. Tutankhamun swallowed up 13 years of his life and left him exhausted.

Even when Carter died, the papers couldn't resist mentioning the "curse" of the Pharaoh in their obituaries. Was it the curse of the dead king that brought Carter and Carnarvon bad luck? Certainly they had no idea what lay ahead that day in November 1922 when they gained their first tantalizing glimpse of the tomb. Perhaps if they'd known, they would have filled in the doorway and walked away, leaving the mysterious Pharaoh in peace.

Further Reading

The Complete Tutankhamun by Nicholas Reeves (Thames & Hudson, 1995)

The Forgotten Pharaoh by Philipp Vandenberg (Hodder & Stoughton, 1980)

The Tomb of Tutankhamun I–III by Howard Carter (Cassell, 1923 – 1933)

Howard Carter before Tutankhamun by Reeves and Taylor (British Museum, 1992)

The Face of Tutankhamun by Christopher Frayling (Faber, 1992)

Howard Carter – the Path to Tutankhamun by T.G.H. James (Tauris Parke, 2001)

Howard Carter and the Discovery of the Tomb of Tutankhamun by H.V.F. Winstone (Constable, 1991)

The Secrets of Tutankhamun by Leonard Cottrell (Evans, 1965)

Acknowledgements

Picture insert

1 Carter and Carnarvon © Hulton Archive/Getty Images

3 Sealed wall with hidden hole © The Griffith Institute, Oxford

2 The antechamber © The Griffith Institute, Oxford

4 The treasury © The Griffith Institute, Oxford

5 Carter and Carnarvon opening the wall © The Griffith Institute, Oxford

6 Tourist watching as treasures removed © The Griffith Institute, Oxford

7 Lunch group in a tomb © The Griffith Institute, Oxford

8 Carter working on the gold coffin © The Griffith Institute, Oxford

9 The gold coffin © The Griffith Institute, Oxford

10 The unwrapped mummy © The Griffith Institute, Oxford

Plan of Tutankhamun's Tomb by Michelle Hearne

Index